4-28-75

Fringe Benefits—
The Depreciation, Obsolescence,
and Transience of Man

WILEY SERIES ON SYSTEMS AND CONTROLS FOR FINANCIAL MANAGEMENT

Edited by Robert L. Shultis and Frank M. Mastromano

Fringe Benefits—
The Depreciation,
Obsolescence, and
Transience of Man—

COSTS, STRATEGIES, AND TRENDS FOR
FINANCIAL MANAGERS, PERSONNEL DIRECTORS,
AND GENERAL MANAGEMENT

STANLEY M. BABSON, JR.

A Wiley-Interscience Publication

JOHN WILEY & SONS, New York · London · Sydney · Toronto

Library of Congress Cataloging in Publication Data:

Babson, Stanley M   1925–
    Fringe benefits—the depreciation, obsolescence, and transience of man.

    (Wiley series on systems and controls for financial management)
    "A Wiley-Interscience publication."
    1. Non-wage payments.   2. Labor costs—Accounting.
I. Title.

HD4932.N6B3   658.1'553   74-13767
ISBN 0-471-03975-6

Printed in the United States of America

10 9 8 7 6 5 4 3 2 1

TO AMELIA

Who many years ago considered Man as an
Investment, and who has these many years
shared my journey through Transience and
Depreciation, and probably some Obsolescence also.

SERIES PREFACE

No one needs to tell the reader that the world is changing. He sees it all too clearly. The immutable, the constant, the unchanging of a decade or two ago no longer represent the latest thinking—on *any* subject, whether morals, medicine, politics, economics, or religion. Change has always been with us, but the pace has been accelerating, especially in the postwar years.

Business, particularly with the advent of the electronic computer some 20 years ago, has also undergone change. New disciplines have sprung up. New professions are born. New skills are in demand. And the need is ever greater to blend the new skills with those of the older professions to meet the demands of modern business.

The accounting and financial functions certainly are no exception. The constancy of change is as pervasive in these fields as it is in any other. Industry is moving toward an integration of many of the information gathering, processing, and analyzing functions under the impetus of the so-called systems approach. Such corporate territory has been, traditionally, the responsibility of the accountant and the financial man. It still is, to a large extent—but times are changing.

Does this, then, spell the early demise of the accountant as we know him today? Does it augur a lessening of influence for the financial specialists in today's corporate hierarchy? We think not. We maintain, however, that it is incumbent upon today's accountant and today's financial man to learn *today's* thinking and to *use today's* skills. It is for this reason the Wiley Series on Systems and Controls for Financial Management is being developed.

Recognizing the broad spectrum of interests and activities that the series title encompasses, we plan a number of volumes, each representing the latest thinking, written by a recognized authority, on a particular facet of the financial man's responsibilities. The subjects contemplated for discussion within the series range from production accounting systems to planning, to corporate records, to control of cash. Each book is an in-depth study of one subject within this group. Each is intended to be a practical, working tool for the businessman in general and the financial man and accountant in particular.

ROBERT L. SHULTIS

FRANK M. MASTROMANO

PREFACE

The title of this book is somewhat provocative and is deliberately so. All too often, accountants think of Man as an element of cost, which he unquestionably is; however, I am not sure that he is as readily thought of as an asset to the industrial enterprise for which he works—an asset subject to the phenomena that affect all other assets, namely depreciation and obsolescence. There is nothing unique in this concept. Man has present direct costs and both present and future indirect costs, and no matter how one may conceive of man, these factors affect the economics of the corporate enterprise, both in reporting of current earnings and in forecasts of tomorrow's expectations.

The objective of this book is to discuss fringe benefits, which are the indirect costs of man. There is already a wide variety of literature on the market on this subject, both in its broadest terms and for each of the major elements of the fringe benefits package. This literature is largely the product of well-qualified authors concerned with social legislation, banking, insurance, and benefit plan consulting. Without detracting from the major usefulness of this literature, the objective of this book is to make what I hope will be a unique contribution, because it is written solely from the perspective of a corporate financial officer for the benefit of accountants and other corporate operating personnel charged with the responsibility of reporting on and forecasting the financial implications of employee benefit programs and decisions. I refer not only to costing of employee benefit programs, but also, and equally importantly, to discussion of the prospect for future impact on forecasted plans for the corporate enterprise in tomorrow's world. It is quite apparent that major trends have been taking place over the past generation in the area of employee benefits. These very changes have had important effects on today's "indirect people costs." Surely no one can doubt that these trends will continue to be a dynamic element for change in tomorrow's world as well. Some of these trends, I believe, can be predicted even now; others can only be guessed at. A further objective of this book is to point out to the various categories of readers, to whom this book is directed, where this trail may lead and what may be the effect on their service to the corporate enterprise along this trail.

I thought that this book was worth writing or I would not have done it. I never expected to be writing a reference book, or textbook, and it is with some little disbelief that I find myself involved in this task now. I have an inbred abhorrence of dry didactic material—with all due respects to many worthy authors of this style. You will forgive me, then, if I depart from the common jargon of such literature, and write the only way I can—the way I think and live and have done so in some 20 years as chief financial officer of various small, medium-sized, and, lately, large, multinational, corporate organizations. I believe you will find the style of this book to be provocative, challenging, and, I hope, imaginative. I don't pretend to know all the answers—I doubt that you will find anyone who does—but to me it is identification of the questions that is the starting point. And that is what I hope to achieve with this book.

I must make one apology to the fair sex in the feminist movement of today's world—many excellent accountants, personnel, and financial executives are not men but women. You will excuse my use of the word "man" in the context of this book—no offense is intended. Perhaps I can explain my use of the word if I borrow from another venerable and worthy profession, the legal profession, which is full of people who are masters in defining terms. While the following phrase is somewhat modified to fit the purpose here, the phrase has always appealed to me as a classic statement of expression:

> the word "man" and the pronouns therefor as used herein shall be construed as masculine, feminine, or neuter and in the singular or plural, as the sense requires.

How could we possibly survive in this world without our friends, the lawyers, to give us such guidance? Perhaps they are a fringe benefit I have not covered in this book.

STANLEY M. BABSON, JR.

June 1974
Tarrytown, New York

ACKNOWLEDGMENT

Special acknowledgment is given to the Actuarial Division of the firm of Alexander and Alexander, New York, New York, for invaluable assistance in providing me with much of the basic actuarial data on which the charts and exhibits in this book are based.

S. M. B., Jr.

CONTENTS

CHAPTER 1

"OH, THE WORLD OWES ME A LIVING"

In the beginning, there was man—and man did not have a guaranteed annual wage; he did not have a minimum wage; he did not even have a salary. Fringe benefits, also, were totally unknown (unless you wish to consider woman as a fringe benefit). Man just struggled for survival and, more often than not, probably did not make it. But this was long ago, before the time of accountants and other financial types.

Eons later, man did concern himself with a salary; at first, it was merely a pittance and not much by today's standards. In retrospect, how many of us like to shock our younger subordinates by proudly boasting that we started out, as a college graduate embarking on a professional career, at $32.00 per week, as if this were some grotesque oddity that we were saddled with in our early years. I have no doubt that 50 years hence today's graduating collegians will similarly boast to tomorrow's future accountants of how *they* only got $12,000 when they started out along the economic trail, again a grotesque quirk of economic fate; and who knows where this very same trail will ultimately lead.

At first, as man entered the industrial environment and started working for a wage, his salary was just about the entire compensation package—maybe some vacation, here and there a holiday, but that was about all. With no idea of pension, man worked until he dropped dead, and in those days the life expectancy of man was far short of what it has become today. Providing for man's sickness was his own risk; his premature death or disability was up to the generosity of his employer. The thought of his employer's providing for his future retirement was unthinkable. And yet, man at this time did not feel unnecessarily abused. This was the natural order of things as he had come to expect and to understand them to be. This was the era of the Emersonian doctrine of self-reliance, where man was independent of the State and chose to remain so. The concept of the Welfare State had not as yet been born.

This is the economic environment in which semimodern man has lived until

1

fairly recently in his time span. All will surely agree that the modern concepts of Guaranteed Annual Wage, minimum wage, shorter working week, and the smorgasbord of fringe benefits, pension portability, vesting, and such are all phenomena of the past 50 years, for even the most rudimentary of them, and of the past 10 years, for the most advanced.

This book deals with the explosion of fringe benefits for man, and, surely, none can deny that there has been such an explosion, as Chart 1 indicates. Fifty years ago, fringe benefit costs of the working man were nonmaterial items to the accountant of those days—not so today. For the accountant who advises his management of the present costs of the operations of the industrial enterprise, these fringe benefit costs conservatively represent 25 to 30¢ on the payroll dollar of additional costs, and bear in mind this is in relation to an everincreasing payroll dollar which in itself represents a dramatic accelerating spiral from what it was a generation ago. Also bear in mind that this 25 to 30¢ covers only

Chart 1. Growth of Employee Benefits as a Percentage of Payroll

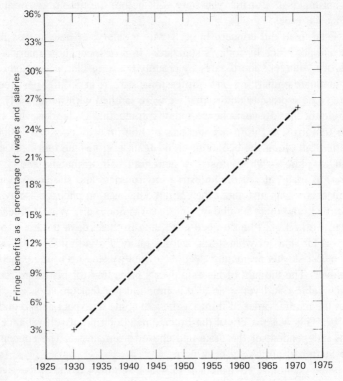

the most basic identified items of direct fringe benefit cost. Chart 2 shows a profile of these most basic fringe benefit elements as they existed in 1971 Department of Commerce statistics.

This book attempts to show not only that there are numerous other indirect costs of significance not normally identified in the captured fringe benefit cost accounting of today, but, also, that in tomorrow's world, tomorrow's accountant has some really significant cost problems facing him in the further explosion of the fringe benefit costs of man.

If this is so, how has all of this come about?

How has modern man emerged from his struggle for survival itself, from his pride in self-reliance and independence, to the philosophy that somehow the State or the industrial organism itself is responsible for the economic preservation of the working man throughout his life cycle from cradle to grave—to the concept that "the world owes me a living"? There is surely a big jump between these two totally different life styles and philosophies.

Unquestionably, the role of unionism has played a tremendous part in this dynamic change, both directly and indirectly. By directly, I mean in across-the-table bargaining. Unions really have a product to sell—security and progress "onward and upward" for their membership. Like many of today's mutual funds, they are and have always been "performance oriented." Either they get something for the rank and file member, something that he could not otherwise get for himself, or they really have nothing to sell. They have been reasonably effective, judging by the results over the years. Indirectly, they have also had an impact because those companies who entertain a horror of unionism and the "closed shop" often seek to head off such a state of affairs by "one upmanship," by being paternalistic to their employees and reducing their need and desire for the protective bargaining that unionism would offer them and they might otherwise find attractive. With the rise of unionism has come the rise in the belief that somehow the industrial enterprise is exploiting the worker and that the balance should be redressed. I am sure this was true a great many years ago in the United States, even as it may now be true elsewhere in the world, but I believe that even the most blind economic observer can see that currently the trend is in the other direction and the "onward and upward" philosophy is in the ascendancy.

This attitude has become politically popular. The impetus to the fringe benefit explosion came with the passage of the initial Social Security legislation in the early days of the New Deal. Since then, as subsequent chapters of this book recite, Social Security costs and benefits have been in a constant and lately increasing perpetual state of escalation. This trend will obviously continue, and the financial planners of today's industrial enterprises had better be aware of the cost implications of this trend and prepare for them. But Social Security is not

Chart 2.   Employee Benefits by Type of Payment, 1971

Type of Benefit	Total, All Companies
Total employee benefits as per cent of payroll	30.8
1. Legally required payments (employer's share only)	6.3
a. Old-Age, Survivors, Disability and Health Insurance	4.5
b. Unemployment Compensation	0.7
c. Workmen's compensation (including estimated cost of self-insured)	1.0
d. Railroad Retirement Tax, Railroad Unemployment and Cash Sickness Insurance, state sickness benefits insurance, etc.**	0.1
2. Pension and other agreed-upon payments (employer's share only)	10.0
a. Pension plan premiums and pension payments not covered by insurance type plan (net)	4.9
b. Life insurance premiums, death benefits, sickness, accident and medicare insurance premiums, hospitalization insurance, etc. (net)	4.5
c. Contributions to privately financed unemployment benefit funds	*
d. Separation or termination pay allowances	0.1
e. Discounts on goods and services purchased from company by employees	0.1
f. Employee meals furnished by company	0.2
g. Miscellaneous payments (compensation payments in excess of legal requirements, disability insurance, moving expenses, etc.)	0.2
3. Paid rest periods, lunch periods, wash-up time, travel time, clothes-change time, get-ready time, etc.	3.4

the sole focus of the political arena of the working man's economics. Minimum wage, while not a fringe benefit, is politically active and will continue to be as a regular diet. Private pension plans, supplementing Social Security, are obviously under close scrutiny, and the concepts of minimum vesting, portability (like Social Security), control of the dollars of the pension portfolio (I am sure that the government would love to control this), and funding of private plans are all now highly political issues. In the society of "Oh, the world owes me a living," and in a society of 200,000,000 Americans, fringe benefits is *big business,* and, as such, become without doubt a major political target.

The evolution of health care as a political tool—we are not yet at the point of full-scale socialized medicine, but we have gone as far as Medicare and Medicaid—indicates that health protection of the working man is as politically at-

Chart 2.   (Continued)

Type of Benefit	Total, All Companies
4. Payments for time not worked	9.2
a. Paid vacations and payments in lieu of vacation	4.8
b. Payments for holidays not worked	3.0
c. Paid sick leave	1.0
d. Payments for State or National Guard duty, jury, witness and voting pay allowances, payments for time lost due to death in family or other personal reasons, etc.	0.4
5. Other items	1.9
a. Profit-sharing payments	1.0
b. Contributions to employee thrift plans	0.2
c. Christmas or other special bonuses, service awards, suggestion awards, etc.	0.4
d. Employee education expenditures (tuition refunds, etc.)	0.1
e. Special wage payments ordered by courts, payments to union stewards, etc.	0.2
Total employee benefits as cents per payroll hour	122.3
Total employee benefits as dollars per year per employee	2544

* Less than 0.05%.
** Figure shown is considerably less than legal rate, as most reporting companies had only a small proportion of employees covered by tax.

tractive to the government as is health care for the aged. In fact, in the July 9, 1973 issue of the Wall Street Journal, an article starts off as follows:

Washington—Without fanfare, the government is launching a $30 million experiment to determine the impact of National Health Insurance on the cost and availability of health care.

Government life insurance for the worker has not been seriously examined, but with so many of our working population already familiar with and covered by government veteran's insurance, it is not a big step from there to more fundamental and far reaching government life insurance proposals.

Outside of the political realm, there is a similar movement in private industry itself that is becoming increasingly more popular. This movement is sometimes referred to as the increasing social consciousness of industry. What exactly does this mean? It means that certain elements of industry, obviously the more liberal avant garde, are becoming aware of a concern about the social problems surrounding us in this country. This concern passes beyond the concern about pensions, sickness, quality of life in the corporate community, and such. This concern focuses on the responsibility of the corporate enterprise to participate in the missionary work itself. This work relates to deliberate programs for recruiting and training elements of minority groups, and not merely placing such personnel "in house" but also attempting to continue such efforts to the point where such minority elements achieve a certain degree of penetration of the supervisory and professional ranks of the industrial enterprise. A worthy endeavor? Of course, it is! Does it have costs associated with it that are indirect fringe benefit costs? Obviously!

The trend goes on. Some say that we are headed toward socialism, and that, in time, the government will control all aspects of the economic lives of the individuals that it governs and that this is the road we travel; it is only a matter of time—who knows?

It is certainly not the function of this book to explore this prospect. Rather, my task here is to recognize, for the benefit of the financial executives to whom this book is addressed, that this trend comes about as a correlary of the already present explosion of fringe benefits in our industrial society. But, more importantly, this trend will continue, and, as it does, not only do its present costs, which need to be understood and properly accounted for, continue, but also they, in turn, accelerate. The objective of this book is to explore with today's financial executives the role they must play in properly accounting for, forecasting, and guiding their enterprises through the trends of tomorrow's Scylla and Charybdis, to which fringe benefits will surely lead us. This is the "onward and upward" society—never doubt it. Wages only go up, not down. There is a life cycle of every industrial product, but there is as yet no awareness of such a life cycle concept as applied to man and his economic value to the industrial enterprise. It is foolish of us not to recognize that man, too, has an economic value, a value which must have its limits in the world in which we live, if we are to live in order rather than in chaos.

Accountants are prone to think of the industrial enterprise as made up of assets and liabilities, costs and revenues. So much of our vocabulary—and every profession has its own peculiar vocabulary—reflects these basic elements. And what of man himself; where does he fit into this vocabulary? Is he, too, not an asset—an asset that depreciates like machinery, an asset that is exposed to the element of obsolescence also, like inventory? And is not man, because of increasing transience, becoming less of a fixed asset and more like a short-term prepaid expense? And is man only an element of cost, or is he a form of investment? The vocabulary sounds familiar, certainly, but are we really accustomed to thinking of man in these terms and relating the recognition of his true costs to the industrial enterprise in similar fashion to these other forms of assets?

The philosophy that "the world owes me a living" sounds politically great, but it has major economic pitfalls for today's financial planners, and these pitfalls must be examined and discussed in some form of comfortable and familiar professional dialogue if we are to be capable of guiding the destinies of our industrial enterprises through what has been called by some, "the age of acceleration." The objective of this book is to do precisely that.

CHAPTER 2

THE DEPRECIATION OF MAN

The commonly accepted definiton of depreciation is "a system of accounting which aims to distribute the cost [of an asset] . . . over the estimated useful life of the asset." * Certainly, the objective to be achieved is a worthy and necessary financial one. However, even under the best of circumstances, as the accountant well knows, there are a wide variety of ways in which even a simple productive asset like a piece of machinery can be depreciated. "Generally accepted accounting principles" of depreciation are not as confined as the layman might think. There could be, and very often there is, a wide divergence in how similar assets, such as simple productive assets like a piece of machinery, will be depreciated by accountants of different financial organizations and all properly within the mantle of "generally accepted accounting principles." Certainly, the estimated useful life of an asset is at best a somewhat subjective determination and often arrived at somewhat arbitrarily, without serious regard on the part of the financial executive to the estimate of real physical life that such an asset may in fact have. Who is to determine over what productive life such an asset will be depreciated—five years, eight years, or ten years? All might be acceptable under the circumstances. This variability can, I think, best be illustrated by reviewing the ranges allowed for certain categories of assets by the new asset depreciation range (ADR) system of the Internal Revenue Service of the U. S. Government. Chart 3 is just one page taken from ADR itself, but serves to demonstrate the point.

Looking at ADR class #34.0, Manufacture of Fabricated Metal Products, it can be seen that the Internal Revenue Service (IRS) itself finds acceptable a determination of useful life for depreciation purposes of anywhere from 9.5 years to 14.5 years.

Is it not fairly obvious that the per annum depreciation charge against earnings for a $40,000 piece of machinery will differ if an estimated life of 9.5 years is selected rather than a life of 14.5 years? Perhaps the differential is small enough taking one piece of machinery at a time, but in the total context

* AIA *Accounting Terminology Bulletin,* No. 1, August 1953.

of all items of machinery, what multiplier changes insignificance and immateriality suddenly to quite a different perspective?

But length of estimated service is only one of the variables of the depreciation equation. "Generally accepted accounting principles" allow a fairly broad variety of depreciation methods ranging from the conventional "straight-line" method to the following more exotic accelerated methods:

Declining balance
Double-declining balance
Sum of years digits
And others

Again, it is fairly clear that the method selected, in addition to the length of life selected, may have a significant impact on the reported depreciation charges against earnings of a given corporation, and, in turn, its reported earnings per share trends. The accounting profession has been less concerned with confining the latitude of choices as with maintaining a consistency of practice between years.

However, these thoughts are not new and are well known to all experienced accountants; but in the context of this book, where man himself is viewed as an asset subject to the same elements of depreciation, are we as familiar with and alert to the application of parallel depreciation accounting techniques as we should be? I suspect that many of us are not. And yet the same problems of cost impact and a wide variety of options exist in parallel fashion, and, if anything, the parameters of variability of depreciation accounting for man are even greater than for more conventional tangible assets.

The working man, too, has a useful life, and his cost during this useful life is not his basic wage alone; it is surely his wage plus the cost of wage continuation after he ceases to make a productive contribution to the corporation.

Depreciation of man recognizes that man will eventually wear out and be taken out of production, and in this instance the cost of supporting him after he "wears out" in the definition of a given industrial enterprise should be identified and recorded over his estimated useful life, that is, his years of active and productive service with the company. This cost, more commonly referred to as his pension cost, is a highly complex cost to measure properly. It is a cost that is subject to a wide range of variables, each potentially impacting quite significantly on the cost of operations of a given corporation, particularly if it is labor intensive. Moreover, certain factors are currently undergoing a subtle yet highly dynamic change which cannot help but be translated into cost accounting problems for the future as well as cost forecasting strategies relative to forward planning.

Let us examine what these pension variables are, as follows:

Chart 3. Section 167 (p. 25,009)—Class Life ADR System

| Asset Guideline Class | Description of Assets Included | Asset Depreciation Range (years) | | | Annual Asset Guideline Repair Allowance Percentage |
		Lower Limit	Asset Guideline Period	Upper Limit	
32.0	Manufacture of stone, clay, glass, and concrete products:				
32.1	Manufacture of glass products: Includes assets used in the production of flat, blown, or pressed products of glass, such as plate safety and window glass, glass containers, glassware and fiberglass. Does not include assets used in the manufacture of lenses	11.0	14.0	17.0	6.0
32.2	Manufacture of cement: Includes assets used in the production of cement, but does not include any assets used in the manufacture of concrete and concrete products nor in any mining or extraction process	16.0	20.0	24.0	3.0
32.3	Manufacture of other stone and clay products: Includes assets used in the manufacture of products from materials in the form of clay and stone, such as brick, tile and pipe; pottery and related products, such as vitreous-china, plumbing fixtures, earthenware and ceramic insulating materials; and also includes assets used in manufacture of concrete and concrete products. Does not include assets used in any mining or extraction processes	12.0	15.0	18.0	4.5

33.0	Manufacture of primary metals: Includes assets used in the smelting and refining of ferrous and nonferrous metals from ore, pig, or scrap, the rolling, drawing, and alloying of ferrous and nonferrous metals; the manufacture of castings, forgings, and other basic products of ferrous and nonferrous metals; and the manufacture of nails, spikes, structural shapes, tubing, and wire and cable:			
33.1	Ferrous metals	14.5	18.0	21.5	8.0
33.2	Nonferrous metals	11.0	14.0	17.0	4.5
34.0	Manufacture of fabricated metal products: Includes assets used in the production of metal cans, tinware, nonelectric heating apparatus, fabricated structural metal products, metal stampings and other ferrous and nonferrous metal and wire products not elsewhere classified	9.5	12.0	14.5	6.0
35.0	Manufacture of machinery, except electrical and transportation equipment:			
35.1	Manufacture of metalworking machinery: Includes assets used in the production of metal cutting and forming machines, special dies, tools, jigs, and fixtures, and machine tool accessories	9.5	12.0	14.5	5.5
35.2	Manufacture of other machines: Includes assets used in the production of such machinery as engines and turbines; farm machinery, construction, and mining machinery; general and special industrial machines including office machines and non-electronic computing equipment; miscellaneous machines except electrical equipment and transportation equipment	9.5	12.0	14.5	5.5

Definition of the pension benefit itself.

Entry age for eligibility.

Age of employee.

Sex of employee.

Retirement age set by company.

Vesting provisions.

Rate of growth of estimated future compensation of employee.

Rate of estimated earnings of the pension trust itself.

Definition of compensation basis for pension.

Mortality expectancy of pension group prior to retirement.

Life expectancy of pension group after retirement.

Turnover expectancy of pension group.

Integration or nonintegration with social security.

Other features such as disability provision, and widows' benefit provision.

Selection of funding method.

Amortization period for past service.

Cost of living escalator.

This list could be extended quantitatively if that fitted its purpose, but the items identified above certainly cover the more material variables that are involved in the determination of pension costs. Before I examine what the impact ranges certain combinations of these variables might have on the economics of the business enterprise, let me first examine the variables one by one to explore how static or dynamic the variable is now or is likely to become in the future, and also how important each variable is in the "pecking order" of materiality of pension cost.

DEFINITION OF THE PENSION BENEFIT

The definition of the pension benefit is certainly one of the most dynamic elements in the pension equation, because it focuses directly on the question of how many years of estimated useful life man will have in the particular corporate environment that he has attached himself to. Obviously, an employee's age must be in relationship to normal retirement age; otherwise, no measurement of useful life exists. More important than a given employee's entry age, however, is the planned entry age that is chosen as the basis for providing a maximum planned pension benefit. If a pension plan is designed to provide for maximum planned pension benefit at age 65 after 40 years of productive life, then this very fundamental philosophy becomes the focal point of pension benefits for that company. This means that if a man joins the company at 25 but does not work until 65, he will have less than full pension benefit from this particular company; it also means that if he joins the company later in his productive life cycle, let us say at 40 years of age, he will not be able to achieve full pension benefit from this company. Obviously, both of these two conditions and a wide range of possibilities in between are happening all the time within a given pension plan and in fact constitute the norm. This means, then, that the normal condition is that few employees today in a given company are expected to earn maximum pension benefit, under the definition specifically set forth above, that is, normal entry age at 25 and retirement at 65 with 40 years of productive life implied.

Certainly, a generation ago the specifications above were not an unreasonable expectancy. People did, in fact, spend all their lives with one company, and did, in fact, spend 40 years working for their retirement benefit. Today, this is not the case, and such specifications are obsolete, but this dialogue is examined in later chapters.

By way of illustration, let us examine the cost differences of providing a given pension benefit at age 65 as we require an employee to work over different variable productive lives. Chart 4 shows, under certain controlled assumptions, how much lifetime pension can be purchased by a 7½% of compensation pension contribution, where an employee works for 10, 20, 30, or 40 years until retirement.

It is obvious from examination of Chart 4 that if 7½% of an employee's pay, compounded over progressively longer increments of productive life, will

Chart 4. Impact of Years of Service upon Pension Benefit— "What will 7% of Annual Compensation Produce?" *

Start-ing Age	Lump Sum Accumulation at Age 65 ($)	Monthly Pension Payable for Life ($)
25	116,071	983.
30	83,576	708.
35	59,293	502.
40	41,148	349.
45	27,589	234.
50	17,456	148.
55	9,885	84.
60	4,227	36.

* Assume a $10,000 annual salary ($833 per month); no salary increases; fund earnings of 6% per annum; and exclusive of Social Security benefits.

yield a curve of this character, concurrently, the cost to the corporation will rise geometrically to provide for such employee a given pension benefit in relation to his salary if the period of productive working life is reduced.

It follows, then, that if the pension benefit is set to provide a certain percentage of an employee's pay at retirement as a socially accepted norm, the cost to the company of providing this same benefit will vary significantly as the socially accepted period of required productive life becomes shorter. Chart 5 shows what the cost will be to reduce the definition of required productive life

Chart 5. Annual Cost of Providing a Pension of $10,000 at Age 65 to an Employee Entering Plan at Various Ages

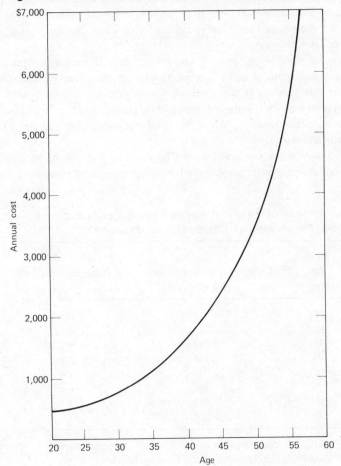

for a given pension benefit, that is, $10,000 per year. (Other variables have been neutralized for this exercise.)

AGE OF AN EMPLOYEE

Within the framework of the dominant variable, that is, the definition of what pension benefit will be earned over what productive time span, the age of a particular employee will determine the company's pension benefit cost for that man and will determine as well his pension benefit within the framework of this particular company. If a conventional formula of $1\frac{1}{2}X$ annual compensation X years of eligible service is used to determine pension benefit, it can readily be seen that a 45-year-old man working 20 years to retirement will earn only 30% of his pay as a retirement benefit, whereas a man age 25, working 40 years to retirement, will earn 60% of his pay as a retirement benefit. Thus while the age of a given employee affects the aggregate pension cost for that employee to the company, it may not directly affect the per annum cost to the company that provides such pension benefit, except, perhaps, in certain indirect ways, and these involve other variables to the pension equation. The variables referred to are the rate of wage inflation projected for an employee and the rate of fund performance for the pension trust. It should be fairly apparent that if the projected wage spiral for an employee is 5% per annum and if the projected fund performance yield of the pension trust is 7% per annum, then the younger an employee is in the plan, the less will be his pension cost to the company in terms of charges against per share earnings of the company; the converse would be true of an older employee. In the case of an older employee, there are fewer years in which to make the net incremental advantage of trust performance work for him. Another variable in which the age of an employee is significant is in the area of vesting or portability as is discussed shortly.

SEX OF AN EMPLOYEE

This variable indirectly affects other more direct variables. It is a widely demonstrated fact that women live longer than men. Therefore, providing for a pension benefit for a woman, all other things being equal, is more costly than for a man. This is covered under discussions of the longevity variable. Women probably impact favorably on the transience statistic because turnover statistics are greater for women than men; this is discussed under the turnover variable topic. Suffice it to say here that sex is a variable in the pension cost formula. If it is true that we are undergoing a social change wherein women will pursue full industrial careers to a greater extent than they have in the past, this factor may well become of greater significance in future pension planning.

RETIREMENT AGE

All known pension plans establish, as one of their parameters, what is known as the normal retirement date—this is the date at which it is expected that the employee will be removed from the productive mainstream, and it is the date at which his pension payments will commence. For some companies this is a mandatory event; for others it is expected, but relief can be obtained usually by Board of Directors' action where extenuating conditions are present. In such instances, it is usually common for the pension benefit to be pegged to service to normal retirement age even if the employee is allowed to remain longer.

A generation or so ago it was quite common to work until 70 years of age; more recently, retirement ages have been set at 65; and, quite recently, there seems to be a noticeable trend toward retirement at age 60. In most plans provision is made for an employee to retire voluntarily at an earlier age with reduced (but not forfeited) benefits. This trend toward earlier retirement dates is an interesting phenomenon; it has definite major impact on pension costs if we consider that accepted norms for retirement pay themselves will not change

Chart 6. Effect of Retirement at Different Ages upon Cost to Company [Assumed: (1) Employee starts at age 30; (2) Employee is to retire with $10,000 per annum pension; (3) Fund earnings are 5%]

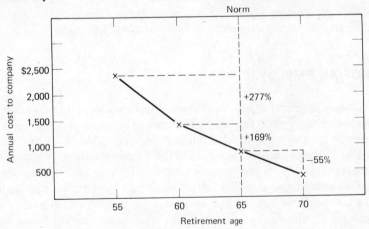

(and I believe it would be naive to think that they would change). If this is true, then, lowered retirement ages mean that a given pension benefit must be provided in a shorter time span of productive life—this can only increase the per annum cost of providing such a pension benefit. Chart 6 demonstrates this point.

It can be seen that a five-year lowering of the retirement age will increase pension costs by 69%.

VESTING PROVISIONS

This variable is quite a significant one, and in recent years has been of particular concern to public officials who have expressed horror at illustrations of employees abused by inequitable vesting features of private pension plans. Simply stated, vesting provisions cover what happens to the accrued pension benefits of those employees who work for a given corporation, but who die or leave prior to retirement itself. What happens to the contribution placed into the pension trust for such individuals? Is all of the benefit which the company has placed into the pension trust for them forfeited by them because they did not stay until retirement, or is all or a portion of such benefit made available to them (i.e., portable), either at death or termination, or kept in trust and paid out to them at age 65? The underlying philosophy of most pension plans in the past has been that the plans are to provide benefits to persons who remain with the company until retirement, and under such a philosphy if an employee dies, it is his group life insurance benefit that is designed to take care of him; if an employee becomes disabled, it is his disability insurance benefit that takes care of him; if an employee terminates to take another job with another company, his retirement becomes the obligation of the other company, and he has forfeited his right to his pension accrual by such voluntary action (this is the "golden handcuffs" concept). There have been numerous instances of hardship by the operation of such a philosophy, and it has been such extreme instances that have rankled in the minds of the lawmakers and public alike, who see corporations placing money into a trust for countless years for an employee and then allowing that money to revert to the corporation when the employee dies or becomes terminated after 10, 20, or even conceivably 30 years of such contributions. Such examples do in fact exist and discredit private pension plans and the corporate image as well in the public view. (Note that the pension contributions do not physically revert to the corporation; they remain in the pension trust, of course, but they do, nevertheless, reduce future contributions which the corporation would be obliged to pay into the trust; hence, the benefit does accrue to the corporation in this manner.)

In more recent years the injustice of lack of vesting has become recognized, and now one usually finds some vesting provision in a pension plan. In my experience, rarely is *full* pension vesting attained before 10 years of employment with the company. Even Congress itself, by its consideration of the proposed vesting concept of the "rule of 50," that is, the combination of an employee's age plus years of service with the company, seems to endorse the principle that pension benefits should not be available in full to short-term younger employees.

It should be fairly obvious that as pension benefits become vested and will, therefore, be paid out to a terminating employee rather than forfeited to reduce future contributions of the company, the costs of pension plans will rise, because corporations will no longer enjoy this systematic windfall gain. Where this trail leads obviously is to vesting provisions becoming more and more liberal in our march toward the "onwards and upwards society," and therefore the cost of the pension benefit itself will particularly increase in parallel fashion.

RATE OF GROWTH OF COMPENSATION OF AN EMPLOYEE

Pension benefits do not relate to present dollars of pay but rather to future dollars of future pay. Some plans, called career average plans, apply a pension formula to an employee's wage each year; in this way his pension benefit keeps pace, after a fashion, with the average movement of his pay over his entire productive career. The cost of these plans is less than for plans which base pension benefits on some form of final pay formula. Such plans usually take the average of the last 10 years of productive employment prior to retirement, or last five years, or highest five years within the last 10, and so on. These plans are obviously more costly to provide—the difference in cost being the inflationary factor of which they take greater cognizance. In the inflationary world of today, and with the need for retirement benefits to track better the inflationary trends of wages and costs, the trend is definitely in favor of final pay plans as opposed to career average plans. This trend will be paralleled by a rise in pension benefit costs to the corporate entity. Chart 7 sets forth for a given controlled employee example, the difference in cost of a career average plan, a final 10-year average plan, and a final five-year average plan.

RATE OF EARNINGS OF THE PENSION TRUST

The economics of providing a pension plan for an employee, simply stated, relate to the amount of money put in the trust each year, which invested at $X\%$

Chart 7. Comparison of Career, Final 10 Year Average, and Final 5 Year Average 1 to 1½% Pension Plan: $10,000 Initial Salary, Increasing 3% Per Year

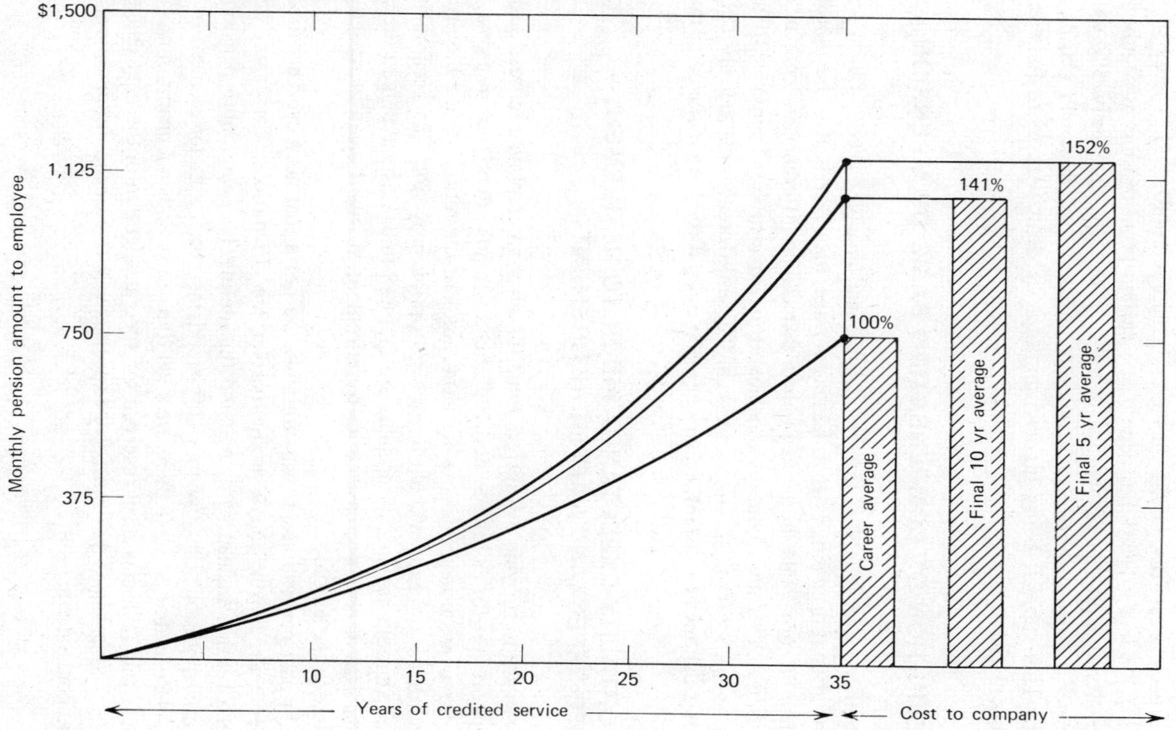

return (interest, dividends, plus market appreciation), and Y years of service, will provide a given dollar benefit at a certain point of time. It should be obvious that under this economic formula, a trust earning only 5% will mean greater annual corporate contributions into the trust than will a trust earning 7%. This subject, being highly important, is dealt with more fully in a subsequent chapter.

DEFINITION OF COMPENSATION BASIS OF A PENSION

Another variable is the employee compensation which a corporation must sustain after retirement. Is it to be basic wage itself, or is it to be more closely related to gross take-home pay before taxes? The difference, of course, consists of bonuses, if any, commissions, overtime, overtime premium, shift differential, possibly profit sharing, and such. These differences can be substantial, and hence can mean substantial extra pension costs if they are included in the base.

MORTALITY EXPECTANCY PRIOR TO RETIREMENT— LIFE EXPECTANCY AFTER RETIREMENT

If we are to provide a wage continuation after an employee retires, designed to support him for as long as he lives, then of major importance as a cost variable of the pension benefit is the life expectancy of the retiree. Some die prior to retirement itself and, without a widow's option provision, the accumulated past contributions for such poor souls are factored in as cost savings to the corporation. If mortality decreases prior to retirement, this will mean increased pension costs to the employer.

In past generations, it was probably the norm that most workers died before they retired from active productive service. In more recent years, men have been retiring instead of dying, and this definitely means more pension cost to the corporation. Because mortality trends are such a major element of pension fund costs and because there are such dynamic trends occurring in mortality tables, this table has been reserved for special attention in the next chapter. Suffice it to say here that mortality expectancy is one of the dominant variables in the pension equation.

TURNOVER EXPECTANCY

Here, again, we have a significant variable and one that is increasing in significance as our industrial society becomes more transient. The employee who spends his entire productive life with one employer is becoming a rarity in today's industrial environment. From a corporate point of view, turnover statistics are only important from a cost element standpoint insofar as they interplay with the vesting provision, and hence forfeited prior year pension contributions that become available for reducing the corporation's future contributions into the pension trust. The transient employee, if he carries no portable pension benefit with him, is a boon to the industrial entity in the world of the recent past, and even of the present. It is doubtful if this inequitable condition will remain for long in tomorrow's world and as it becomes obsolete, as discussed in the chapter on transience, it will signal major rises in corporate pension costs.

INTEGRATION WITH SOCIAL SECURITY

When Social Security legislation first became a reality back in the 1930s, those advanced corporations who were sufficiently socially conscious in those days to have any pension plans at all were somewhat concerned as to the future trend of mandatory pension contributions into a government fund. By way of protection, it became common practice to integrate public pension benefits into the planned benefits of corporate private pension plans. This practice in reality meant that private pension benefits were designed to provide a certain retirement benefit to an employee *inclusive* of what he might get from Social Security itself. This meant that if Social Security benefits should go up, as would be expected of a politically concerned program, then conversely, the amount of benefit to be provided by the private plan would be commensurately automatically reduced. The rationale for this was reasonable enough, because corporations feared that if they did not avail themselves of this protection, their pension costs, taking public and private sector together, could skyrocket beyond their control. Social Security was of course a law that mandated certain corporate and employee annual contributions expressed as a percentage of payroll up to certain levels. This action on the part of corporations was, therefore, entirely defensive and was really understandable. A later chapter deals specifically with the trends of Social Security over the past number of years.

While in recent years many plans have been initiated which do not integrate with Social Security, it should be fairly obvious that the fact of integration versus nonintegration has quite a considerable bearing upon the cost to the company of its pension benefit.

SELECTION OF FUNDING METHOD

Another dynamic variable is the selection of funding method for determining annual contributions into the pension fund. In simple terms, the choice between

funding methods is the choice between (*a*) paying currently for future inflationary demands of rising wage levels which would tend to stabilize pension
costs from year to year given a relatively static experience of change in employment roster, turnover, and such; and (*b*) paying for future inflation needs
"as you go," which entails obviously increased pension costs each year, and
which must be met regardless of whether such cost increases will be stra-
tegically desirable in a given future year if profits in such year are depressed.
These two basic funding methods are referred to as "attained age" and "entry
age" methods, and their impact can best be shown in Chart 8.

It should be remembered that the pension benefits in Chart 8 are the same,
and the costs are also the same. It is only the timing of recognition of costs that
is the variable here. The argument for the one method is that pension costs are
known and therefore can be planned without surprise or embarrassment. This is
a more conservative method. The other method may seem more logical to the
accountant, because it follows in theory the philosophy of matching the income
with the expense. In this instance, the inflationary rise in pension expense is
presumably to be met along with other inflationary cost increases by a commen-

**Chart 8.   Effect of Funding Methods (*Total* shaded area repre-
sents "initial actuarial liability" arising from an average employee now aged 42. Only vertical shaded area is "true past
service cost".)**

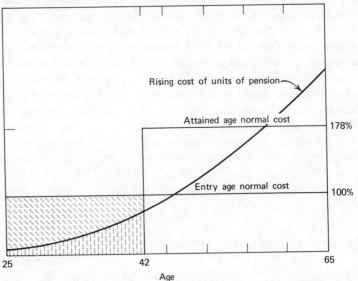

surate inflationary rise in the corporation's sales prices of its products. If this is strictly followed, expense matches income, and no financial pinch or embarrassment occurs. In my experience, however, things do not often work out this neatly, and if prices cannot be readily increased, rising planned pension costs can be an unattractive bargain and a millstone around the corporate neck.

AMORTIZATION OF PAST SERVICE

Past service may arise with the initiation of a new pension plan where none existed previously. An existing roster of employees at a given point of time may well be given credit for years of prior service with the company before the inception of the pension plan. This is called past service, and its costs may be computed as a lump sum and charged to income of the corporation over a stream of future years rather than as a period expense in the year of creation of the plan. All that pertained to establishing the useful life of a piece of machinery, pertains to the selection of a reasonable period of time over which to amortize past service pension costs.

OTHER FEATURES OF PENSION PLANS

There are a great number of other features that can be written into pension plans, almost all of which have cost additive elements and some of which have material cost elements. Such provisions are widows' options, disability, and cost of living escalations, to name a few. But I feel the point of diminishing return has been reached, and that the more important variables have been identified previously in this chapter, or as indicated, are treated, because of their significance, in separate chapters to follow.

ACCOUNTING CONSIDERATIONS FOR DEPRECIATION OF MAN

The discussion above of the relative importance of various variables involved in the pension benefit for man lends perspective to the dynamic parameters of this element of cost. Now we must try to put these variables into some perspective that can assist the financial executive, first in accounting properly for the cost of the benefits that have been designed and agreed upon, and second in projecting for his management the probable changes in future costs that may lie ahead.

I think it would be helpful to divide the variables discussed above into two general categories:

1. *Design variables*, which are inherent in the fundamental benefit provisions agreed on.
2. *Operational variables*, which operate independently of design features and can accelerate or retard the cost impact of the plan itself upon the earnings performance of the company.

It should be apparent from the earlier discussion that the design variables should be critically examined prior to implementation if present costs and future cost trends are to be properly known and controlled without surprise. Once these design variables are solidified, it is safe to assume that you are "locked in" and that "you can not go home again"; it is only "onward and upward" as further design changes come about over the years either in response to union bargaining, to employee need or to outside competitive pressures. The design variables would include the following:

Definition of pension benefit
Retirement age established by the company
Vesting provisions
Definition of compensation base
Integration or nonintegration with Social Security
Disability provision, widows' option provision
Cost of living escalator, and such

Operational variables would include the following:

Mix of the employee body as to age and sex
Rate of growth of future compensation
Mortality tables
Turnover tables
Selection of funding method
Amortization period for past service
Pension fund earnings performance

These latter variables can be monitored by the financial executive throughout the operating years of the plan's existence, and they obviously should be, or the executive could be considered derelict in his responsibilities. Obviously mortality tables cannot be controlled; however, the corporation's mortality experience can in fact be minimized by a careful prehiring physical examination; employee turnover rates can definitely be influenced by corporate policies, as can the rate of growth of future compensation (within limits). Of greatest concern is the variable of the earnings experience of the pension fund itself. The financial executive is extremely remiss in his duty if he takes a passive view of this factor. As regards funding methods, amortization of past service, and even projected fund earnings performance, these variables can be changed by the financial executive if in his judgment such changes are defensible. Until recently, his ability to change variables almost at will was virtually unchallenged. However, with the advent of the American Institute's Accounting Practice Bulletin (APB) 8, this is no longer so. The essential thrust of APB 8 is that if actuarial

Chart 9. Profile of a Pension Cost

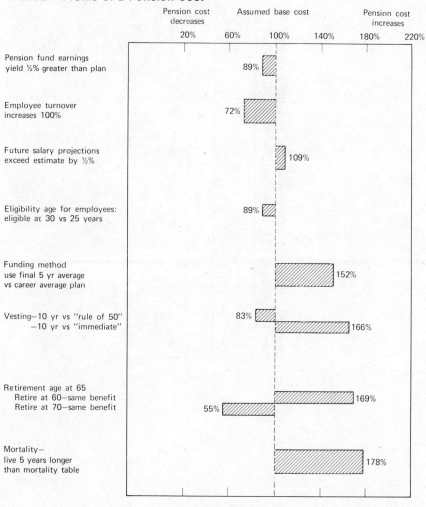

Chart 10. Illustrative Parameters of Variability of Pension Plan Costs upon XYZ Company (Based on Chart 9)

Plan Design Features (Basic Plan Cost = $675,000)

	Downside	Upside
1. Eligibility	$675,000	$675,000
Restrict from 25 to 30 years	×89%	
Extend to all entrants		×238%
	$600,750	$1,606,500
2. Vesting		
Change from 10 yrs. to "rule of 50"	×83%	×166%
Extend to all	$498,600	$2,666,000

Plan Operational Features (Basic Plan Cost = $675,000)

	Downside	Upside
1. Fund earnings improve ½%	$675,000	$675,000
	×89%	
	$600,750	
2. Turnover doubles	×72%	
	$432,500	

3. Salary increases are ½% more than projected		× 109%
		$735,750
4. Funding method, final 5 yr. average vs career average	$432,500	× 152%
		$1,118,000
	$432,500	$1,118,000
	$216,250	$559,000
	$216,250	$559,000
	8.6¢	22.4¢

Subtotal	$498,600	$2,666,000
tax effect at 50%	$249,300	$1,333,000
after tax	$249,300	$1,333,000
EPS	10.0¢	53.3¢

Note: Retirement age, mortality, and method of spreading costs in early years have been omitted from this profile because these variables would only distort the comparisons above (in the same direction) even more provocatively and perhaps might exaggerate the parameters that are normally available and variable to the financial executive.

variables are legitimately altered, the variance so created may not be absorbed in one given year but must be spread over a period of years. This concept is obviously designed to discourage short-term strategy treatment of the accounting for pension benefits by diluting the benefits themselves insofar as they can permissably impact upon a given year.

In summary, I think perhaps the best way of illustrating the dynamics of design variables and also of operational variables is to show how they could affect earnings per share of XYZ company under certain extreme choices that are available to the alert financial executive. Let me introduce you to XYZ company.

XYZ Company

Annual sales volume	$30,000,000
Gross profit	50%
G&A	10%
R&D	3.5%
Selling and promotion	20%
Profit before tax	16.5%
Profit after tax	8.3%
Return on net worth	15%
Payroll percent	30%
Payroll dollars	$9,000,000
Price earnings ratio	10X PAT
Number of shares outstanding	2,500,000
Earnings per share	$1.00
Market price of stock	$10.00
Theoretical market value of company	$25,000,000
Number of employees	1,000

In Chart 9, I have attempted to show a "Profile of a Pension Cost," a rather complex and elusive phenomenon. While the factors supporting this profile are valid enough, nevertheless they do relate to fixed and arbitrary assumptions which may or may not be present in any given pension study. Therefore, please do not take this profile in a manner other than which it is intended, that is, to show the reader how different elements in the pension equation can impact on the cost to the corporation under a given set of circumstances.

In applying this illustration to XYZ Company to show the dimensions of the decision-making opportunities available for consideration, Chart 10 attempts to put Chart 9 profile into an earnings per share context.

SUMMARY

In summary, I believe I have presented in this chapter what I believe to be an almost bewildering array of considerations for the financial executive to consider in his approach to the accounting for costs and cost variable opportunities relative to pension plans. These I have provocatively suggested are nothing more than an alien vocabulary for the depreciation of man himself. Man is such an important asset in the environment of the industrial enterprise that the accountant should not allow himself to presume that the economics of decisions bearing on his depreciation costs are the province of industrial relations personnel or manufacturing operations personnel alone. There is too much at stake for this attitude, and the depreciation costs of man can only become more material in the future, as I have attempted to suggest, and for this the financial executive must be properly prepared and alert to the challenges of tomorrow.

CHAPTER 3

THE OBSOLESCENCE OF MAN

Obsolescence is defined in the *Accountant's Handbook* as "resulting from development of more economical methods of production, frequently due to radical changes, or new inventions resulting in greater efficiency and lower costs, and sometimes due to new legislation which may render the continued operation of the old assets unprofitable or impossible, or sometimes due to changes in economic conditions."

The concept of obsolescence of man is a bit difficult for the ego to swallow. But be that as it may, with all due respect to egoism, the facts clearly point in the direction that man, as a corporate asset in today's accelerating age of technology, is definitely subjected to the risk of obsolescence before he is fully depreciated. Most accountants have seen this phenomenon with regard to other assets, notably machinery and equipment, and, more particularly, with product inventory itself. It is often not simply "wearing out" that requires such assets to be withdrawn from productive life before their normal and potential life span has run its course. Equipment may be replaced by new generation models that perform the same functions more efficiently, faster, more economically, with less maintenance, and so on—all of which means that the corporation cannot really afford to continue the old generation asset in service. With product inventory, the product life cycle may be short-lived, and its demand lagging; new competitive products may usurp its economic or technological attractiveness in the market place. The result is obsolescence. Equipment is retired from service and replaced with new generation equipment; inventory is scrapped out or otherwise disposed of. In both instances, residual asset values are written off to costs of operations at the point when the awareness of obsolescence is recognized.

But we would like to think that man himself endures, that man adjusts perhaps, but nevertheless, endures, to the end of a normal physical depreciation. While this may have been true some time ago, I am afraid that it is no longer the case. Top management executives, who a generation ago were not considered ready for top level responsibilities until they were at least 60 or 65 years of age, now find that the philosophy and practice of corporate management seeks younger and younger men to guide the corporate helm. Virtually unknown a generation ago, the corporate chief executive of 45 years of age is now becoming not only familiar, but also more and more the norm. Stockholders to a greater degree are now seeking younger men with higher energy levels, with fresh imagination, and with access to higher technology familiarity than had their predecessors of the past. This same trend is pretty much true down through the roster of management levels in virtually all areas of the industrial enterprise. Younger engineers are closer to the technology explosion of our scientific universities. While a generation ago it may have been sufficient to be an electrical engineer, a physicist, a chemical engineer, a mechanical engineer, now only a nuclear physicist will suffice, or an expert in fiber optics, in microbiology, in laser beam technology, and so on.

How many of yesterday's CPA's are comfortable in today's computerized MIS systems, and do they feel at home with COBOL, FORTRAN, and RPG? Has yesterday's marketing manager kept abreast of simulated models of market penetration studies under different economic programs? Does he even know today's "buzz" words?

By way of illustration, let us look at a few case histories—ones that I have come in contact with through the years:

1. Financial executive A has worked almost from inception of his company until it has now grown to $8,000,000 in annual revenues. He is not a trained accountant, but because of his age (age 50), maturity, judgment, and years of service with the company, he is the top financial man. He has one junior accountant working for him and a lot of clerks. He relies heavily on outside auditors to do the "accounting thing." He essentially controls supervision of cash receipts handling and cash disbursements. His company is acquired by merger with a larger company. Outside auditors are changed, and a major public accounting firm is brought in to streamline the systems and procedures, set up mechanization, establish a cost system, recruit a qualified controller, and such. A young controller, age 30, is hired to be Chief Financial Officer, and now Financial Executive A reports to him. The question arises, "What can Financial Executive A do; is he really obsolete?"

2. Chief Financial Officer B, age 42, is managing the financial function for a $50,000,000 retail company, dominated largely by buying functions, merchandising functions, and cash flow. Essentially, he is serving as Treasurer of a straightforward operation. Through a quirk of fate, his Chairman brings in a dynamic new Chief Operating Officer, one who

aspires to aggressive growth via acquisitions, movement into foreign markets, change from retailing into manufacturing operations, and movement concurrently into R&D and product development. You can guess the result; conservative plodder Chief Financial Officer B is no longer able to cope with the newly defined needs of the company under this new leadership. He is seen as a negative person and an obstacle to growth, and is eventually discarded and replaced. In this instance, he is replaced not by a younger man, but by a man whose experiences, perspectives, and technical skills are more in line with the changed needs of the company. Here, again, B is obsolete.

3. Chief Engineering Officer C, working for a small manufacturing company, has been with it since inception; he designed the early products, simple first-generation models, which were all manually operated. He is not a young man; he is over 60, and he spends more time thinking about all the things that he has done in the past than he does about the things he wants to do in the future. Mechanical engineering is his "bag." Electronic engineering? Chief Engineering Officer C is not at home with this new field or able to contribute effectively to its technology. He knows that it is the technology of the future. His management comes to realize that this is the reality and hires a bright young crackerjack of an electronics engineer, age 28, and very bright. New product ideas soon become focused on electronics, and this new man soon becomes the dynamic focus for forward product development. Because he is vocal, capable, and aggressive, it does not take long before he is Vice President of Research, and the old Chief Engineer is a senior retired consultant on his staff. Another case of obsolescence.

4. One final illustration is of an inventor, founder of his company. He conceives of an interesting idea, develops it, markets it, and it catches on. He is off and on his way. Because he is charismatic, egoistic, and dynamic, and has a good product, he speeds along this path toward a successful company growth pattern. The early years are tough; he first makes the product in the cellar, later in a small warehouse, and finally, in a complete manufacturing plant. As in the case with many similar ventures, the growth curve starts out fairly flat; then it rises slowly almost arithmetically; then the geometric curve enters and rapid growth spirals upward. The company is now at an exciting phase; investment bankers are eager to take it public and do so. The track record looks dynamic and promising. But what happens? What happens, in this case, and often in other parallel cases as well, is that the founder soon finds that the life of a $15,000,000 public company with worldwide activities, tax exposures, insurance risks, SEC do's and don'ts, and foreign currency and bank credit problems, is

far more complex than he possibly imagined. Furthermore, with success comes the corollary of recognition by potential competitors who soon enter the field and not only try to catch up but also try to "leap frog" ahead in terms of technology. Our inventor now is faced with a dilemma; namely, this company he has created now demands of him more skills than he has to offer. If he is smart, he will recognize this at an early date and take steps to bring such skills on board and give them the share of responsibility that they require. Regretfully, this often does not happen, and egoism and pride of invention create barriers to change until the company is in trouble and belatedly faces the inevitable—that its founder himself is obsolete.

So much for illustration; these all are very real cases, and I am sure no reader of this book will have to think very far afield before he will recognize similar examples in his own experience. They exist on a broad basis in our present industrial life.

Technology and technique are changing rapidly before our eyes. Rarely can the older man keep up with this explosion and hope to compete with youth and innovation. And what, then, is the result? The result is obsolescence.

If this is true, then, can today's financial executive ignore the economic impact of such an obsolescence factor in recording the current true financial position of his company and, more particularly, can he do so in his role at economic planning for the future? The answer is, obviously, no, he cannot.

Before we examine what to do about recognizing and cost effecting this factor of obsolescence, let us review some statistics which confirm the observations which I have made thus far. Chart 11, repeated from, Chapter 2, shows that if obsolescence occurs and man does in fact retire younger and expects a comparable retirement benefit as at age 65, the cost impact to his corporation will be significant. Chart 11 indicates that the corporation can expect to pay a 69% premium for this social phenomenon.

It is quite apparent from studies of professional recruiters that the profile of the corporate chief executive officer is steadily turning toward younger candidates, and I would presume that the parallel trend would exist with other top management posts as well, (see Chart 12). If this is so, a fairly obvious question is, "What happens to the older men of top management talent—those who have passed beyond the profile range?" Obviously, no simple answer exists that would fit across the board, but generally the answer must be that such men retire earlier and take themselves out of productive service with the corporation, or else the action may be initiated the other way around. It would appear from the statistics that there is a noticeable trend toward earlier retirement, and I feel confident that a serious statistical study would show that this trend is largely

Chart 11.   Effect of Retirement at Different Ages on Cost to Company [Assumed: (1) Employee starts at age 30; (2) Employee is to retire with $10,000 per annum pension; (3) Fund earnings are 5%]

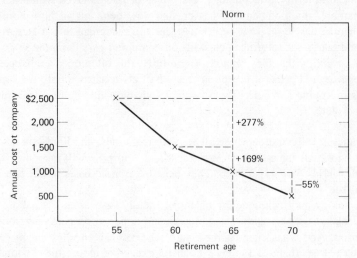

centered on the higher and more affluent elements of management. Today's corporate management pace is more demanding of its participants, and it is also more rewarding to them financially. These men have "made their pile," taken their turn at the power structure of the corporate hierarchy, and are probably glad to step down, while life and a reasonable amount of energy still exists, to reap the fruits of the industrial system that they have plowed. To the extent that this is true, then, the obsolescence fact is voluntary and serves a useful purpose both to the individual himself and probably to the corporation. The fact that a major asset power is now rendered nonproductive, thus representing an element

Chart 12.   Age Profile of an Industrial President

Present Age	1972(%)	1967(%)	1962(%)
Under 50	28.1	25.1	22.0
50 to 59	57.2	52.6	43.0
60 and over	14.7	22.3	35.0
	100.0	100.0	100.0

of inefficiency in our capitalistic system, has not as yet appeared to concern anyone to any significant degree.

If obsolescence, particularly of the higher paid corporate personnel, is in fact becoming a more dynamic factor generally, then must not this somehow impact adversely the costs of the corporate enterprise? Surely obsolete inventory that must be written off to cost of operations is a familiar and more often than not distasteful problem that the accountant faces, unfortunately probably on a regular basis. Most adept accountants faced with periodic "baths" or write-offs of inventories that have become obsolete anticipate these traumatic experiences by providing for reserves on a "pay as you go" basis. Where a certain element of risk of exposure to obsolescence exists fairly continuously, it is certainly not an improper course to set up reserves through monthly charges against income. In this way, the periodic write-offs will be cushioned by being charged against such reserves rather than appear as comments in the corporation's annual reports—"The fourth quarter results were depressed due to extraordinary year end adjustments, etc., etc." You all know the language, I am sure.

Well, what about man as an asset? How do we handle his cost of obsolescence? If it is a voluntary early retirement, then the pension plan picks up the tab for part of his wage continuation, but surely not enough to trigger voluntary retirement. This could only occur if a very liberal pension plan is designed or achieved by amendment, one that takes care of the executive needs over a shorter time span so that he can afford to retire prematurely. If this is the case, then the cost of obsolescence is really the extra cost of providing for a given pension benefit at age 55 or 60, instead of at age 65. Such a cost would be accounted for over the productive life of the employee as his normal pension cost.

It should be quite apparent from a review of Chart 11 that the economic impact of obsolescence cannot be ignored. There are surely significant cost differentials involved. If obsolescence is confined to a relatively small percentage of the total roster of the corporation, then, conceivably, its aggregate relative impact on the total company may be diluted, but as this percentage increases, the obsolescence cost will become commensurately more pronounced.

Changing the specs of the pension plan itself to accommodate obsolescence is only one way of providing a sufficient retirement benefit at an earlier date. Probably the most dynamic way is in the area of executive incentive plans, a subject which is covered in a later chapter. Liberal executive incentive plans serve the function of rewarding successful participants, often with benefits that are major in significance. When such happens, it obviously provides the mechanism for early retirement, for going off and enjoying "one's pile", and for a variety of other mechanisms of removing the executive from his productive cycle with the industrial enterprise. In some instances, this is beneficial for all parties. It allows the executive to enjoy the fruits of his energies, sometimes paid for at high personal sacrifice, other times obtained, unfortunately, more through windfall than through merit. It also allows the corporation to move up younger men to positions of responsibility, which, if they are available in the organization, is not only desirable, but also fundamentally necessary. But, in some instances, this mechanism works against the corporation and deprives it of a needed talent, and perhaps exposes the corporation, in instances where no cadre of young hopefuls is being groomed for top management roles, to a deterioration of management. While instances of this latter condition do happen, it is more the trend of the times to welcome obsolescence (when disposed of) as generally beneficial to the corporation.

Whichever device serves as the mechanism whereby obsolescence can become implemented in the corporate enterprise, the result is the same; somehow the obsoleted executive can afford to step out of the productive mainstream earlier than planned. This can only come about at a cost to the corporation itself, and it is this cost that the financial planner should be aware of, as it becomes more pronounced in the increasing trend toward greater obsolescence in the industrial environment.

And where will obsolescence stop? Will early retirement at age 55 be the magic figure, or will even this figure itself change downward in the future? In theory, should not the obsolescence mean age correspond to the ever-lowering average age of corporate executives themselves? It would certainly seem so to me. And do we really believe that this search for youth and energy in the management profile has gone about as far as it can go? I think the answer to that is no. In the age of acceleration of the industrial society, the demands to be met by the corporate executives of this industrial society will of necessity have to be met by increasingly younger persons. Hence the search for youthful talent to take command will continue in the future, and tomorrow's curve will be a further continuation of the trend line that I have already alluded to earlier in this chapter. If I am correct in this premise, then surely I am equally correct in pointing out the likelihood of a parallel lowering of the trend line of the age of obsolescence. That this will have even greater cost impact on the economics for tomorrow's corporation seems fairly obvious. Whether the phenomenon of obsolescence remains confined to the top 10% of corporate executives or becomes generally applicable to a wider span of older employees is debatable and remains to be seen. Perhaps the determining factor will be whether it is the pension benefit which provides for obsolescence, or whether it is the executive incentive benefit. If it is the pension benefit, then the same benefit will be equally available to all persons covered by the same plan, but in proportion to their compensation levels, of course. In this case, the 50 year old foreman with 30 years of service may decide to retire and enjoy life—not because he is obsolete, but because he is tired of working at the same job, and he can now afford to retire. The same philosophy could apply throughout the entire corporation. It just

Chart 13.   Base and Incremential Pension Costs After Taxes —Effect on Earnings per share of XYZ Company of Retirement at 60 Rather Than 65

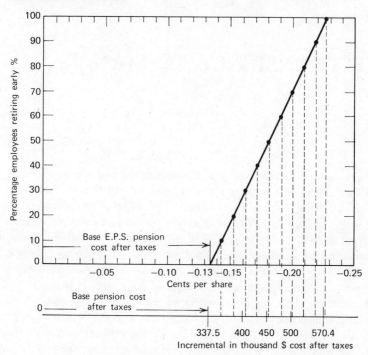

may become the popular norm to retire earlier and leave the industrial environment. There is evidence to suggest that this may well be the direction of things to come. If this is true, then economically, obsolescence or early retirement, will be the norm, and the larger cost dynamics will apply. And how will our XYZ corporation look in tomorrow's world of obsolescence? (see Chart 13)

As financial executives, it can be seen that XYZ company may be in for some pretty rough days ahead. It may well be that before we are through this book we may conclude that man is a pretty expensive asset, perhaps too expensive for tomorrow's corporation to afford.

And what of our people who retire earlier? What of man himself? How will obsolescence affect him? This, I believe, will become one of the big sociological issues of our next generation, as man withdraws from the Industrial Society to become part of "the drone society," a society dedicated to consumption rather than to production.

CHAPTER 4

THE TRANSIENCE OF MAN

Conventional accounting concepts of depreciation and obsolescence of fixed assets of a corporate enterprise are well known to the financial executive. The purpose of this book, as already indicated, is to have the accountant conceive of man as a similar corporate asset subject to parallel concepts of accounting for depreciation and obsolescence. But man has an additional dimension that is not quite parallel to other conventional asset accounting theories; namely, man is subject to the additional phenomenon of transience or impermanence. The commonly treated corporate asset is acquired for a cost. It is depreciated over its physical life cycle, or obsoleted at an earlier date, and finally, when exhausted, it is disposed of for salvage value. This is not so with man, at least not in today's modernized and much more mobile industrial environment. The days when man joined a business enterprise and committed his energies to such enterprise for the duration of his productive life, which was the norm two generations ago and common even in the past generation, are in today's world far from usual. Man today is transient. He is mobile and is becoming more so with each passing year, and, indeed, in the very near future it may well be a rarity to find a man who has dedicated his working life to a career with one single corporate enterprise.

The emergence of such transience has added a new dimension of cost identification for the accountant. Employer turnover statistics, recruitment costs, relocation costs, severance pay policy, unemployment compensation experience factors, use of overtime versus increased employment, use of subcontract temporary help are all highly pertinent topics in today's industrial society. They are not just topics for the industrial relations department alone. They all involve costs, and often quite significant costs, and consequently, they are of vital interest not only as a proper accounting concern but, far more importantly, as a concern of the financial executive in advising management in the areas of financial planning itself.

WHY IS MAN BECOMING MORE TRANSIENT?

Perhaps a better question is why is man no longer bound by permanence? It was his motivation once to tie himself to a job almost always "until death us do part." This was particularly true away from the large metropolitan areas. Contributing to this permanence were lack of transportation and an absence of a variety of alternatives. If you have only a handful of opportunities to choose from, the likelihood of your accepting your lot is far greater than would be the case if you were confronted with an ever-widening assortment of choices, many often challenging you to change.

Therefore, transportation, density, and availability, I feel, play a definite role in increasing incidence of transience.

A second factor may well be a Keynesian multiplier effect that argues that monetary advancement can be accelerated more rapidly by moving externally than by moving internally. I am not sure that this has been factually demonstrated to any widespread degree, but the thesis seems highly likely in the absence of the "golden handcuffs" motive, considering basic salary advancement alone. This, of course, would apply more to exempt salary classifications, that is, white collar rather than blue collar workers, although I am sure job mobility to seek greater wages and fringes is still a key factor in blue collar ranks too.

A third factor seems to be surfacing these days, and that is just plain job boredom itself. People seem to require a greater degree of novelty in job experience than they used to. Many articles have been written recently by industrial managers on the subject of different approaches to relieving worker boredom with repetitive operations—music has been tried, as have radical deviations from progressive assembly line philosophies where economics of specialization are well demonstrated. Even this well-proven bastion has been challenged by boredom as experiments are being run in many places now to depart from specialization, and opportunities have been given to assemblers to perform a variety of operations, even to the point of assembling an entire unit personally. The objective is to achieve a greater sense of job satisfaction, hence motivation on the job. But why should this be important unless it is to improve quality or reduce transience?

Aggressive young junior executives on the rise are not as concerned with boredom however. In their case, the building block effect of job experiences is the road to acceleration of advancement, and money and status are the motives, not boredom. And where in all this is company loyalty? Does it exist? I am afraid that the only honest answer to this is that it is declining in importance as a basic and primary motive.

Chart 14 shows a profile of turnover statistics used as guidelines by the actuarial profession in the calculation of the costs of pension plans. Of course,

Chart 14.   Basic Actuarial Turnover Statistics (other than mortality) per 100 employees

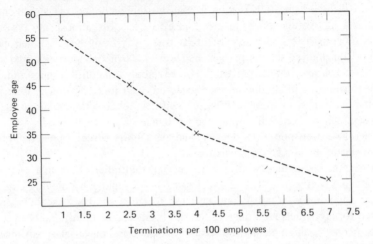

these statistics are generally modified in specific plans to fit the confirmed experience trend of an individual company, because it is a company's own statistics which will govern its performance and hence its costs, rather than generalized statistics of the world at large.

Attitudes are also changing to keep pace with this changing phenomenon. Many years ago the number of jobs an applicant disclosed on his resumé was a critical element in the initial decision of whether to interview him. I myself have discarded many an accountant's resumé in the past on the basis that he was "a job hopper" with no record of job stability. Today I am not sure that this is the case any more. It is true that the job movement record is examined and is important, but the quantity of jobs is not held so critical now as is the quality of the experience. One negative remains, at least in my mind, in screening an applicant, and that is the average stay on a job. Job stays of 4 or 5 years do not alarm interviewers any more, but job changes in a year and a half or less obviously do. Why should this be so? It is so, I believe, because increasing transience is becoming recognized and accepted in our modern industrial life style. It is only the more exaggerated risks that we attempt to screen out now.

In a recent survey of accounting resumes, the statistics shown in Chart 15 were compiled:

Chart 15 is the profile of transience. It suggests that many of our modern industrial employees are highly mobile. It also seems to suggest that mobility is even more pronounced in the younger age groups than it is in the older ones. If

Chart 15.   Profile of Employee Turnover *

Age Group	Average Number of Jobs Held	Average Length of Time Jobs Held (years)
Under 30	2.4	2.6
Age 31 to 40	4.0	3.8
Over 40	4.5	5.7
Average of all ages	—	3.7

* Statistics taken from a random sampling of job applicants in 1973.

this is true, then, one might conclude that transience is not only quite evident but also accelerating.

WHY IS TRANSIENCE IMPORTANT?

Transience is important for several reasons to the financial man:

1. Turnover of employees is a significant factor in determining the cost of a company's pension plan. In Chapter 2 we discussed the fact that termination of an employee prior to attainment of full vesting under the provisions of a given pension plan resulted in forfeiture of benefits by the employee. Forfeiture of benefits by the employee carries with it, in most instances, a cost reduction benefit back to the company, at least indirectly, in the reduction of future contributions that the company will make into the pension trust. Chart 16 attempts to demonstrate the potential impact upon turnover and forfeitures on the basic pension cost of a company.

Following this illustration, there is the implication that the more mobile our industrial society becomes, the more private pension plan costs may be reduced. This may well be true to the extent that forfeitures of unvested pension benefits accrue to the company's benefit by way of reduced future company contributions into the pension trust. But such logic, nevertheless, is somewhat illusory, in my opinion, because it implies that transient industrial man is content to forfeit repeatedly his pension benefit in favor of mobility. I do not believe that this will be the case. Man will want to retire in any event, and if his retirement benefit will not be provided in the private sector, then he will either bring pressure through his congressional representatives to change the portability of pension benefits in the private sector (and this is currently of major

Chart 16.   Effect of Forfeitures on Pension Cost to the Company [Assumed: (1) Employee starts at age 30; (2) Planned retirement at 65 a $10,000 per annum pension; (3) Fund earnings are 5% per annum]

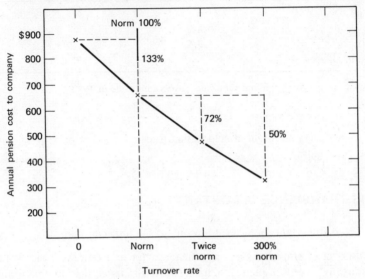

importance on the Congressional scene); he will bring pressure on the public sector to provide larger benefits via social security (and this, also, is being done currently and has been a rather continuous process over the years, and will undoubtedly continue so in the future); or he will exert pressure for improvement in *both* the private sector and the public sector at the same time (and this is being done and seems to be the direction things will undoubtedly go). The result of all this cannot be *reduced* costs to the corporation, even though, superficially, it would seem so in the short run.

To place this in perspective, let us examine the effect of a turnover acceleration on our XYZ Company. Let us assume that XYZ Company has no dramatic turnover event like a layoff, but, rather, has a general increase in turnover statistics of its roster of personnel from 1% per month to 2% per month. In the short-term, this trend change would probably not be reflected in the actuarial calculations, but when it became fairly apparent that the trend was a recurrent norm, then it would be proper to take it into consideration. When such a change is reflected, it will have the effect shown in Chart 17 on the annual pension cost of XYZ Company.

In spite of the somewhat arbitrary assumptions of this illustration, it should

Chart 17. Employee Turnover Rate Effect on Pension Costs and Earnings per share of XYZ Company [Assumed: Normal turnover rate equals 10% of total employed, which represents base pension cost of $675,000 (pretax) and $337,500 (after-tax), or the equivalent of −13.5¢ per share]

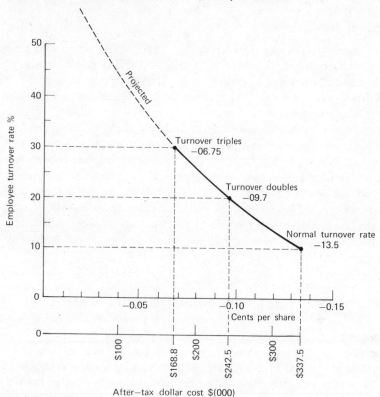

be fairly obvious that forfeitures, taken alone, can greatly impact on the costs of the company. Hence transience must be considered as a dynamic element in the equation of accounting for the costs of man.

2. A second reason why transience is important is that turnover of employees involves other costs, as well as penion costs. It costs to recruit an employee, to interview him, to relocate him, and to train him until he is efficient, and, if terminated, his severance pay after productive contribution ceases provides a further distasteful and costly epilogue to the "employee mistake." And how does the accountant recognize these costs? Does he aggregate them and

call them "costs of employee turnover"? Nothing as useful or imaginative as this is done. Instead, old Mr. Green Eyeshade records:

Personnel Department—salaries
Advertisements
Agency fees
Moving costs

Or the moving costs may show up in T&E accounts elsewhere, and severance pay would probably be recorded in Salaries and Wages of the cost center that the terminated employee no longer serves. Training costs are probably buried in Salaries and Wages or Direct Labor of the department in which the employee was assigned.

Is this really a misstatement of reality for most of us, or are we financial men telling our managements what it really costs to bring a man "on stream," and what it really costs to lose him and start all over again? And nothing has been said yet about unemployment compensation costs. When an employee is tired of it all and has pulled a little ahead of the game, he can quit and coast for awhile on unemployment pay. Never for a moment doubt, Mr. Accountant, that *you* are picking up the tab for this post productive wage continuation. And it is not a two weeks severance package, but about 26 weeks of wage continutation payments.

WHAT DOES IT COST TO RECRUIT AN EMPLOYEE?

It should be fairly obvious to the accountant that it costs money to recruit an employee just as it costs money to issue a purchase order, to type a letter, to carry inventory, and to install and place in service a piece of machinery. It would be interesting to know, however, how many accountants can tell their managements what it costs to hire an employee and bring him to his work assignment. We would probably be startled to learn how few of us can really cite such figures with any substantial data to support our calculations. And yet, why should such costs not be readily measurable? Why are they less measurable than manufactured product costs, R&D project tasks, and such, which we go to elaborate pains and expense to measure properly? Can we possibly believe that accounting for the costs of man is not equally as dynamic and important to the fortunes of our company as these other costs? How foolish it seems to set up elaborate accounting concepts and measurements for fixed asset additions, retirements, and depreciation for a company that is labor intensive rather than capital asset intensive and to ignore the far more fundamental accounting challenge of people cost. Sophisticated inventory cost accounting systems measure direct labor in considerable detail; they measure indirect labor costs, also, in a variety of ways:

Rework
Repair
Waiting for work
Clean-up
Union-management meetings
Moving material
Set-up
Inspection

All of these costs relate to the nonproductive costs of a direct worker. These are costs that the cost accountant finds financially meaningful and worth considerable attempt to measure, inasmuch as they represent necessary but additional people-cost directly related to actual effort directly applied to the creation of product.

Why then are we also not interested in the following?

Cost to Hire

Cost to authorize a new hire.
Cost to locate candidates.
Cost to interview.
Cost to examine, for example, medically, references, and testing.
Cost of agency fees, if applicable.
Clerical cost to add to payroll and benefit plans.

Cost to Move

Cost to look for house.
Temporary cost of living expense while looking.
Transportation costs of moving employee and his family.
Cost to relocate household goods.

Cost to Train

Cost of orientation.
Cost of initial rework, rejects, and scrap.
Learning curve cost—labor efficiency variance.

Cost to Terminate

Cost of severance pay.
Cost of Unemployment Compensation (if applicable).
Cost of termination interview.
Clerical cost of removal from payroll and benefit plans.

This appears to be an impressive array of costs! Perhaps they are individually incidental and minor, but in the aggregate they amount to a sizeable sum and one that should not be passed by. It is easy to think of the Industrial Relations Department or Personnel Department as another service department with an overhead that must be absorbed along with other elements of administrative overhead of the corporation. This is simplistic. The Personnel Department incurs a large percentage of its budget in costs such as those identified above. These are not fixed costs. They are *variable costs,* and if the corporation experiences an upsurge in its business which requires an accelerated recruitment program, these costs will rise and could well rise significantly. Do we as accountants measure the costs of a surge in employment versus the costs of alternative means of increasing production, that is, extended use of overtime and greater use of outside subcontracting? Surely these cost comparisons must be made and viewed against the risk factor of time duration of the need. If we accountants are not doing this cost/risk justification analysis, we are failing in the performance of our role as financial advisers to management. Man tends to be a "committed cost," and a rather adhesive one at that. Accountants have been trained to think in terms of direct labor as being directly variable with production, and supervision and indirect labor as being semivariable, and management salaries as being fixed. I do not subscribe to this simplistic view at all. Direct labor rarely varies directly with production. Once direct labor is hired and in place, it becomes as much a committed cost as the next labor element. When production declines, direct labor itself does not decline automatically; it is productivity that declines. Momentum lags; workers tend to stretch out the job in the absence of piecework standards or other forms of industrial engineering efficiency measurements. Managements are not unaware that this decline in productivity occurs; more often than not, they silently concur with it and procrastinate, hoping for a turnaround in business that could reverse the condition. It is only when the procrastination period ends, and management decides on a layoff that direct labor becomes variable. In the blunt jargon of the accountant, it is only "bodies out the door" that reduce costs and conserve dollars. It is not the purpose of this chapter to discuss the variability of direct labor, but it is well worth more thought than commonly found in the academic textbooks. Our concern here is the awareness that there are important costs associated with the decision to either hire or terminate employees, costs that are above and beyond the direct outlays for salaries and wages, costs that are beyond even the obvious direct fringes themselves. These additional costs cannot be ignored.

Up until now, this section has dealt conceptually with the identification of these additional costs. Can we attempt to quantify them?

In reviewing available literature on this subject, the diversity of views is amazing. Dean B. Perkins, in his article entitled, ''The Doomsday Job—The Anatomy of Turnover,'' has set forth the following survey of costs:

Employment expenses. These include all direct and indirect costs associated with hiring. Some theorists maintain that only employment costs associated with separations and replacements should be calculated since even a company with no turnover adds people because of expansion and a company must maintain the employment function regardless. The cost schedule as conceived of here, however, charges the entire employment function to turnover, whether employment activity is related to internal expansion or replacement. The function is then prorated among hires, reinstatements, and rehires.

1. Advertising expense for recruitment purposes.
2. Printing charges for company publications such as benefit booklets.
3. Agency fees.
4. Search fees.
5. Costs of selection or prescreening, including physical examination, testing, and reference checking.
6. Travel costs of candidates.
7. Travel costs of recruiters.
8. Wages and salaries of employees whose primary responsibility is in the employment function.
9. A reasonable proportion of wages and salaries of employees who spend only part of their time in the employment process.
10. Wages and salaries of those involved in the interview process and in subsequent directly related meetings or decision-making conferences.
11. An allocation of office supply costs.
12. An allocation of normal overhead expenses.

Breaking-in costs. This factor consists of all expenses for supervisory and nonsupervisory personnel in connection with on-the-job training of a new employee. Breaking-in costs can range from $125 to $200 for the average clerical, technical, or hourly production worker and are $350 to $375 for the average salaried nonexempt employee.

1. Wages and salaries of supervisors and key nonsupervisory personnel engaged in on-the-job training.

2. The cost of materials and equipment directly associated with on-the-job training.
3. The cost of the production time lost by a nonsupervisory trainer from his usual responsibilities.
4. Wages and salaries of people maintaining learning curve statistics and other associated record keeping.
5. Wages and salaries of those developing materials to be used in on-the-job training if other than the supervisor.

Startup costs. These are the costs of substandard work performed by a new employee. For production workers a conservative estimate is $330, for salaries nonexempt employees about $650, and for clerical and technical employees about $250. Startup costs continue until the employee's productivity reaches the average employee output for the same job.

Training costs. These include formal classroom training expenses, not on-the-job training, which is usually accounted for under breaking-in costs.

1. Wages and salaries of training personnel.
2. The cost of materials and supplies used in the training class.
3. Normal overhead expenses prorated among the number of people trained.
4. The cost of orientation and tours.
5. The cost of special seminars held away from the place of work for training and development.
6. Tuition aid and reimbursement for education outlays.
7. The cost of renewal programs such as cycling sales training and technological updating courses.
8. Costs associated with retraining transferred or promoted employees who subsequently leave.
9. Miscellaneous expenditures—on name tags, refreshments, photographs, and so forth.

Separation expenses. They include costs incurred as a direct result of an employee's separation from the company. On the average the expenses run approximately $200 for a production worker, nearly $300 for an office or technical worker, and a bare minimum of $600 for exempt personnel.

1. The cost of production lost during recruitment for a replacement.
2. The cost of productive equipment down time.
3. Wages and salaries of all personnel working on the separation, including employees carrying out exit interviewing, terminal processing, and payroll and credit union record keeping.
4. Severance pay.

Short-timer costs. These costs are quite difficult to measure; an estimate may be all that is possible. However, it is worth the effort to isolate them. They include all costs attributable to the behavior of employees who plan to quit.

1. The cost of the employee's reduced productivity.
2. The cost of the reduced productivity of fellow workers due to time spent with the terminating employee in conversation and farewell.
3. The cost of the employee's time away from work for job hunting.
4. The cost of the employee's time spent writing resumes and using company facilities to reproduce and mail them.

I quote all of this text because I think Mr. Perkins has covered the subject fairly comprehensively. He has failed, nevertheless, to indicate an aggregate figure for the sum total of these expenses. Other sources have been more sanguine.

A recent AP (Chicago) newspaper article, headlined, "Firms Pay $2,280 to Move Executives," referring to a survey conducted by Atlas, one of the nation's largest moving firms, indicated that "twenty per cent of the companies we surveyed moved their executives about once every two years. A third of the companies moved people once every five years."

A recent survey by General Telephone Company of Michigan and G&E Laboratories pointed the high cost of recruiting and training at "$14,000 to recruit and train a cable splicer."

Dr. Robert W. McMurry, in "Tested Techniques of Personnel Selection," published by Dartnell, included the following:

A national manufacturer in the textile field found that it cost the company $2,195.92 every time it had to replace an experienced machine operator.

A radio manufacturer reported the following cost of turnover for a semi-skilled plant employee:

Hiring cost	
Advertising	$ 24.00
Interviews—physical exam	28.30
Testing—placement	11.26
Paperwork	15.08
Training	178.90
Extra spoilage	64.20
Extra supervision	91.02
	$412.76

Termination cost

Production lost	$ 59.80
Exit interview	14.04
Paperwork	17.18
	$ 91.02
Grand total	$503.78

A large manufacturing firm with an extensive executive training program found it could scarcely afford to guess wrong on trainees. By the end of his second year each man represented an investment of well over $30,000! And this investment was totally lost if the man left or proved unsatisfactory. Here is how this company broke down its costs for each trainee:

Recruiting (newspaper display ads)	$ 1,440.00
Screening an average of 603 candidates and interviewing an average of 67 candidates (80 hours at $20 per hour)	1,600.00
Checking references (includes cost of an average of eleven long-distance calls)	146.52
Clerical work	134.96
Salary—(not fully productive for 2 years—charge three-fourths 1st year, one-half 2nd year)	16,500.00
Travel expense for field training (estimated)	6,000.00
Training cost—2 years (executive time, materials, etc.)	9,960.00
	$35,781.48

The costs of selection errors varied from company to company for different jobs, but they were always high.

It is obvious that these views are appropriate, but all over the lot. It should be apparent, however, that the economics of transience, particularly of short-term need employees, cannot, I repeat, *cannot,* be overlooked by the financial executive in his views on utilization of man as an asset to meet short-term needs of the corporation.

CHAPTER 5

OTHER PERIPHERAL
COST CONSIDERATIONS

We have discussed that man depreciates, becomes obsolete, and is also becoming highly transient, all of which carry definite current financial costs as well as future economic planning consequences for the financial executive. What else is there for him to be aware of? As a marriage that begins with the promise " 'til death us do part" (depreciation) may end in divorce (obsolescence and also transience), the vow "in sickness and in health," is part of the protocol. The same is true with industrial man. The corporation that he throws in his lot with is supposed not only to pay his living wage, provide for his retirement either through obsolescence or depreciation, but provide also for the following:

Disability.
Premature death.
Accident on the job.
Sickness—cost of hospital, medical and major medical bills.
Sickness—protection for wage continuation while unable to work productively for the corporation.
Accident while travelling on company business or accident away from the job, even, not on company business.
Fatigue—i.e., vacations, holidays, and sick days.
Employee recreational activities to increase his morale.
On-the-job training to learn how to qualify for a better job.
Academic improvement via tuition reimbursement plans.
Cafeteria subsidies.
The phone bill as a "fringe benefit."
Employee discount on company products.
Other "quality of life" conditions.

Is there anything I have left out? Frankly, I doubt that I have even scratched the surface! This chapter, while entitled "Other Peripheral Cost Considerations," attempts to assess the more significant of these various incidental factors that enter the working man's economics. Never doubt that they are part of today's reality. Never doubt that they each have costs, costs which, in isolated instances, may seem trivial, but in the aggregate cannot be ignored by the accountant.

From an accounting standpoint, these costs do not appear to present much of a problem, certainly not in the same class as the more prominent cost elements earlier discussed. Many of them are covered by insurance programs, and costs therefore are leveled out via regular insurance premiums charged against income on a monthly basis, with extraordinary charges, if such occur, borne in the first instance by the insurance carrier, not by the company. All of this sounds quite simple and straightforward from an accounting viewpoint. But is it as mundane as it appears, or do challenges lurk here for the accountant to examine?

First, there is the philosophical problem, not of accounting for these costs, but of reporting them. How many accountants aggregate them under a common expense section so they can be readily tabulated and related as a fringe benefit to the costs of man? These items should definitely be recorded as fringe benefit costs rather than insurance costs. I do not believe there is any significant disagreement with this premise or with the reporting of such costs in this manner, for that matter, but there are an assortment of peripheral costs which are not so widely recognized as "people costs," and which, therefore, might not ordinarily be accumulated as part of the fringe benefit package.

For instance, how many companies classify travel accident premiums as an employee benefit rather than as a cost of general corporate insurance? How many companies recognize that personal use (or abuse) of the corporate telephones does, in fact, occur on a regular basis, pretty much from top to bottom of the corporate status scale? Does not this item have a cost that admittedly may be difficult to measure but is more closely reported as an allowed fringe benefit cost than as an ordinary telephone expense? Can any accountant doubt that telephone credit cards in the possession of traveling field men are used for occasional personal calls as well as legitimate calls to customers?

How many companies allow the use of company-leased vehicles as a so-called perquisite? Are these rentals classified as a fringe benefit or are they treated as ordinary travel and entertainment costs?

I would be willing to wager that the Xerox machine, or its equivalent, sees a fair amount of personal use in most companies, costs which are lost under either "stationery and supplies," "purchased services," "equipment rentals," and so on.

And do we really know how much lost time for sickness and occasional absence costs the company? With hourly workers who punch the clock, the answer is "Yes, we do," but not with the exempt and salaried categories of employees. For some inescapable reason, it is beneath the accountant's dignity to measure loss of productive time for such employees, and it is invariably buried in basic salaries and wages which is presumed to be fully productive. The theory for this is that such sums would be paid anyway, so what would be gained in attempting to isolate this data? It would not save the corporation any money. This logic eludes me, for, while it is superficially correct, I cannot help wonder why the accountant does not think his management would be interested in knowing how many nonproductive man-days were paid for with no direct value received. And was this part of the employment bargain? True, it is unlikely that management will deduct lost time increments from the salaries of exempt and supervisory employees, but such lost time must be directly equivalent to an excess of manning needed by the corporation, or must be matched by an increase in needed man hours through other sources, perhaps additional roster of exempt personnel. In my simpleminded view, if there are 20,000 man-hours of administrative work to be done, then 10% or 2000 lost man-hours must be replaced by either overtime, at a premium, or by the hiring of an additional person. If this is accepted as logical, then the 10% lost time is not properly reported under salaries and wages, which implies productive usage, but under some appropriate lost time category. The accountant who fails to identify such people inefficiency cost is really not discharging his optimum responsibility to his management. And how do we account for discounts on employee purchases of company product where relevant? Not as an additional fringe benefit, I would bet.

This list could undoubtedly be expanded considerably. It is not my purpose here to identify an exhaustive roster of peripheral cost considerations, but merely to alert the financial executive that they do exist and that they are in reality fringe benefits, and most importantly, that it is his job responsibility to tag them and report them in a manner which is constructive for the needs of the management of his corporation.

TO WHAT EXTENT IS COST CONTROL POSSIBLE?

Most financial executives are a breed of maverick that will just not accept costs which appear to be wasteful. While on the surface, many of these peripheral costs may seem to be inescapable, like "death and taxes," some opportunities for cost controls do exist and the financial executive should be aware of these, if he is not so already.

Workmen's Compensation

This cost is familiar to all accountants who normally charge the monthly insurance premiums to expense as a period charge. This is a very simple solution but in itself may not be enough. It is true that Workmen's Compensation administration and claims processing is technical and complex and should be left to professionals. Many of the larger corporations find it economical to establish their own in-house professional staff of Workmen's Compensation administrators, but this is the exception rather than the rule, I think. Certainly in smaller and medium-sized firms this course would not be justified. Be that as it may, it is of considerable importance, nevertheless, to receive regular experience reports from the insurance carrier as to paid claims and reserves for future possible claims. Not only do such reports provide valuable and necessary guidance for strengthening the corporation's safety programs, but, more fundamentally, they alert the financial executive to the appropriateness of the insurance premiums that he is paying to the carrier. Contrary to a rather naive and widespread view among many financial men that insurance at a minimum gives a company protection and at a maximum affords an opportunity to "get something for nothing," I do not subscribe to this view. Over the long pull, I believe it is more realistic to assume that "you pay for what you get," and that, in reality, over a period of years, you are paying for your own claims cost plus an administrative fee for the professionalism, risk-taking, and profit of the carrier. Certainly this view is appropriate for the lesser catastrophic elements like Workmen's Compensation, medical insurance, automobile, disability benefit, and group life. Areas where it is less likely to apply are fire, U&O, and product liability.

It is not my purpose to propose a debate on the nature of insurance; rather, my purpose is to point out to the financial executive that in most areas of fringe benefit insurance plans, there should be a reasonable correlation between claims experience plus administrative charge, and the premiums paid to the carrier. Unless the financial executive is aware that this is so, he may charge off to expense needless extra costs beyond what is appropriate. Let us take, for example, the illustration shown in Chart 18.

It should be obvious from Chart 18 that the corporation involved has paid premiums for these years substantially in excess of what was a proper cost to the company. Nevertheless, the accountant for each of these years paid the premiums and charged them off as period expenses each month perhaps without challenge. These are to a certain extent unnecessary costs and, once incurred, cannot be recouped. What should be done? The financial executive of the company in Chart 18 has two choices of action:

Chart 18. Relationship of Workmen's Compensation Claims Experience Versus Premiums Paid for Specific Company "A" (shaded area represents paid and accrued claims)

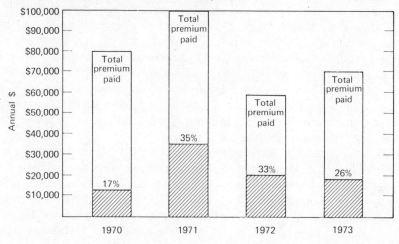

1. Switch to a policy with a retrospective rating provision. This means that when the policy period is up, the premiums paid will be adjusted to reflect the actual claims paid and reserved, plus an administrative charge (probably somewhere around 14% depending on size of premiums).

2. Go into self-insurance; retain a professional firm specializing in Workmen's Compensation administration to handle claims administration and claims control, and purchase a high deductible catastrophy umbrella policy. Where a large number of employees are in a single location, this latter plan might be advisable, but it is less attractive with multiple factory locations around the United States. Various local laws also may complicate this alternative in some states, but it can be done. It has an additional advantage of improved cash flow over and beyond the basic claims cost itself.

Medical Insurance

Medical insurance is one of the most important fringe benefits that a company can offer these days, because with the high cost of medical bills these days, a serious health problem can cause a real hardship to the average employee, and with semiprivate room rates per diem approaching $100.00 per day in major metropolitan areas, *any* employee medical insurance is a highly nervous and emotional social issue. If you doubt its emotional impact on your rank and file, try to change their plan. Once you give a certain level of benefits, you "can not go home again." Here is one area where you must do your homework in advance. Do not buy benefits carelessly; the cost "comes home to roost." At the outset, you must identify your corporate philosophy. Do you really want to buy front-end dollar-for-dollar coverage or do you want to buy insurance?

If you want to buy front-end dollar-for-dollar coverage, and you have a sizable group of employees in a single location, you may wish to self-insure. You are not buying insurance, but a cooperative financing plan, and you can probably administer that more cheaply than to pay an outsider to do it, unless you wish to shift "the bad guy" image to a third party.

If you want insurance, then insure very well against the serious risks and set up a high major medical deductible to eliminate the numerous small dollar petty bills that a family should normally pay for anyway. Only they can control these bills; you can not and never will effectively. The only point I wish to make here is that what benefits you contract for are quite important in medical insurance. Your per-employee cost can well run the gamut of a $100.00 per employee differential per annum; for 500 employees this is $50,000 per year—certainly important enough to give some serious thought to in advance of decision-making.

And do not forget "coordination of benefits" clauses. It may seem trivial superficially, and it is highly unpopular with labor unions, but this clause can be very important and it is widely misunderstood. In simplest terms, it means that where more than one carrier insures an employee's family medically, *one* carrier will pay the claim, not both carriers, when a claim is processed. There are elaborate rules for determining the "after you, Alphonse" procedure of the carriers involved. The objective of the insurance carriers here is to reimburse your employee. Unfortunately, many employees, and the unions which represent them, feel that medical insurance is like a lottery; if you "pay your money" (or your employer does, which is almost always the case), you collect. If both the husband's and the wife's employers pay separate premiums with separate carriers, then each carrier would pay and the employee's family would collect twice. Is this the benefit you really want to give your employee?

Group Life

Group life plans have been very cheap insurance and quite efficient, and because the rates are so attractive, they look like a real bargain for employers. All of this, I believe, is true. There is no doubting that the rates that are available under group plans, particularly where there is a sizable group, are extremely attractive when compared with rates that an employee would have to pay as an individual outside the group. But again, I urge the financial executive to examine the correlation between his claims experience and his premiums if he has a large group. If he has a small group, then, most certainly, he cannot consider self-insurance, but the larger the group, the closer should be his correlation between premium and paid claims.

In a later chapter, I talk about another aspect of group insurance; namely, that we, as employers, are being deluded by the attractiveness of the rate itself in buying benefits which in themselves are inefficient and wasteful.

One further thought for the financial executive to examine in group life insurance is the possible redundancy of premiums for the same benefit under different forms of coverage. Is death benefit being covered under the pension plan as well as under group life? And if so, is this efficient, and what was contemplated? Better examine it.

Wage Continuation Plans

This benefit, like medical insurance, is another highly emotional social concern. What employee does not worry about the prospect that sickness or accident may incapacitate him temporarily? Medical bills are one thing, but having the pay check continue to come in to pay the rent and food bills is every bit as important. It seems strange to me that medical insurance plans seem to have been given more prominence and publicity than have wage continuation plans. The two are inseparable to me. The risk in both plans, however, lies in the delicate balance between adequately and legitimately protecting an employee from hardship and making it relatively unattractive for him to return promptly to work to resume his productive cycle. This is a real dilemma, and, as every insurance carrier will advise you, there are serious cost considerations involved.

And how are we accounting for sick pay? Before any wage continuation insurance takes effect, there is a "front-end waiting period." This operates much as a deductible feature does in other types of insurance coverage, and it usually comprises the first continuous week of illness. The company pays for this, certainly, in continuing the paycheck of its exempt personnel, and, perhaps, to a degree, for some of its nonexempt personnel as well. Is this front-end money left accounted for as "salaries and wages," or is it reclassified as sick pay? Obviously, the latter treatment is highly desirable whether it is payment for an isolated sick day or two here and there, or whether it is for the full week prior to the takeover of the insurance policy. But while the reclassification of such payments out of the "salaries and wages" account and into "sick benefits" may be an administrative nuisance, the visibility to management is worth the effort. I am afraid that in many companies this visibility on the true cost of sick pay is not available but is lost in what is presumed to be productive wages.

Unemployment Compensation

Too often accountants, and perhaps, even personnel men, tend to think of unemployment compensation insurance as a routine insurance and straight-forward cost. Its premium is easily identified and accounted for. The burdens of administration have been shifted to agencies outside the company, and cost control possibilities are not given much attention. But cost control opportunities do in fact exist and should not be overlooked. This topic has been discussed in the chapter on transience, so I try to avoid redundancy here. Regular experience reports from the various State Unemployment Compensation Commissions must be obtained and examined carefully. Prior even to these reports, all claims for unemployment benefits should be examined promptly, and if a protest is to be filed with the Commission it must be done so before the time period for doing so expires and benefits are awarded by default. While cost control opportunities do exist at this level, the best place to control costs lies in the area of employee selection, employee morale, and reduction of the impact of employee turnover itself. This is the area for the Personnel Department, obviously, but the financial executive must be satisfied that adequate steps for cost avoidance are being taken. This is a never-ending vigil.

Fatigue

Under fatigue I have listed vacations, holidays, sick days, and such. Holidays are the easiest to control because the plant is closed. Vacations are easy to control too, if you pay attention and bother with reporting controls. But sick days—trouble! Again, I have to refer to exempt categories only, because, by and large, in my experience, sick day absences of blue collar workers are generally well-documented and controlled, thanks somewhat incongruously to Wages and Hours laws. But how much documentation is generally kept on "exempts" and how reliable is it? How many sick days has John's secretary really had and was she really sick? And how do you police it, and do you really care? The answers to these questions vary widely from company to company, and so do the costs involved. How good a guy do you want to be? Chances are, if you want to be a good guy, you are costing your company money.

Combating Obsolescence Itself

I have already pointed out that obsolescence is a potential disease that even now increasingly lies in wait for many of today's employees. And yet, recognizing this would almost presume that we owe our employees who are exposed to this risk some additional benefit that we might call "obsolescence protection." Is there such a thing? And, if so, how much does it cost and how much is it worth?

On-the-job training is certainly one form of such protection, but I believe most such programs relate more directly with increasing a worker's productivity than with reducing his risk of obsolescence. Tuition reimbursement programs would be more in line with this problem, I think, because here we are not as much concerned with short-term productivity gains as with long-range skills development. And yet, is not it true that for the most part these programs, which are quite common in our corporate environment, deal with the younger roster of employees? This being true, we can not claim this as obsolescence protection for these employees. They can not have been even remotely concerned with obsolescence as yet; in fact, we are accomplishing the reverse, actually, because by financing and encouraging these younger men to expand their skills access to academic technology we are in reality *accelerating* the exposure of their older associates to the risk of obsolescence. And yet, encouraging youth is surely considered to be a socially desirable employee fringe benefit.

But how to attack the problem of risk of obsolescence for the older man? I believe that one possible serious answer to this lies in the application of the concept of a "sabbatical" to the industrial environment.

I am sure the reader is familiar with the concept of the sabbatical as it applies to the academic world. Hard working industrialists have for years secretly envied their academic counterparts for this major respite from the toil of the task, but in vain. Industrialists, being bound by the confines of the pragmatic, have never been able to conceptualize effectively how an executive would be removed from the corporate mainstream for a sufficient period of time to make a sabbatical a realistic and viable option. Undoubtedly, this is some form of egoism, which I am sure many observers will brand as entirely unjustified, but such has been the case in the past. Oddly enough, there seems to be some noise in the air these days about industrial sabbaticals, and it could well be that this noise will fall on increasingly receptive ears. Certainly an industrial sabbatical of months or even a year could be a sufficient interval of time, if properly structured, to enable an obsoleting executive to renew himself in some form, or to reorient his direction if this be his choice—both strategies might be highly beneficial to himself and to his corporation. This is avant garde, as of now, but I personally believe it is coming, and when it comes, it will be the only serious present response to the problem of approaching obsolescence. Even so, however worthy, the program will involve additional peripheral costs.

Phone Bill, Xerox, Stationery

"These areas are small potatoes," but the same comments apply as with absentee days. If you want to be a good guy, chances are you are costing your company money. And, below the surface, are these really such small potatoes? Suppose each of your 500 employees makes two personal local calls per day. Sound unrealistic? It is not! Let us assign a modest 15¢ local charge per call. This means 30¢ per day per employee (not counting his or her lost time, the cost of your switchboard personnel, a secretary handling busy signals unproductively, and such). The cost, then, is as follows:

500 employees (total annual payroll of $5,000,000) × 30¢ per day = $150.00 per day × 240 days = $36,000 per year = $7/10$ of 1% of payroll or almost 4¢ per hour per person

Small potatoes? Maybe, but add Xerox and add stationery and supplies and add a host of other things, equally small potatoes, and before you know it you are in a quicksand of mashed potatoes all around you!

What to do about it?

How do you control these costs? How do you get people to be aware of it and to care? This is the heart of the problem, and there is no easy answer. It seems to be fundamentally true that the overwhelming bulk of our employees have no serious idea of their real cost to the company and whether they are cost effective or not. This has been a "no-no." But this attitude is just not good enough in today's real world. We are competing in the world market place, and in area after area we are losing out. Have we priced ourselves out of the effective market place in spite of our massive productivity lead time and advantage? If we have done so, and I believe we have, it is because we have let our "people cost" get out of control. And this has happened because our accountants were too busy "counting beans" and worrying about accepted accounting theories, and such, and have abdicated the area of constructive, imaginative financial reporting on what was going on around us and where this trail would lead.

If this is true, and if my evaluation is remotely correct, can we do anything about it? The answer, I believe, is "yes, we can." We can at least tell our employees what their *real* cost to us is. They will never know it unless we tell them. In recent years, many of the more progressive corporations have been starting down this trail. They give employees an annual statement of the benefits—the whole roster of benefits (or at least the most meaningful ones) that their corporation is giving to them. I am sure that the common reaction of employees when they receive such a statement for the first time is one of amaze-

Chart 19. Annual Statement of Benefits for John Doe

Your Retirement Benefits

When you reach your normal retirement at age **65** on **APRIL 1, 2000** you will be eligible to receive an estimated monthly income of:

$380   from your Retirement Plan.

$303   from your estimated Profit Sharing.
        Account of **$48,243.**

$284   from Social Security.

$967   is your total estimated monthly income.

$135   is the additional estimated income from Social Security which your dependent spouse will receive from **HER AGE 64.**

$153,594   is approximately what it would cost you to provide all of the above monthly income on your own.

Your Medical and Hospital Benefits

For You and Your Family

Basic Hospital—Surgical Plan

100%   of eligible expenses for semi-private room and board for a maximum of **365** days.

100%   of eligible regular hospital expenses incurred.

80%   of all covered doctor's charges.

Maternity Benefits (if applicable)

80%   of covered doctor's charges for Normal Delivery.

80%   of covered doctor's charges for Caesarian.

80%   of covered doctor's charges for Miscarriage.

Major Medical Benefits

80%   of all covered expenses in excess of **$100** (your deductible) and not paid for under the Basic Plan.

$15,000   maximum benefit in any 12 month period.

Your Sickness and Disability Benefits

If you become sick and disabled and are unable to work, you will be eligible, after exhaustion of Company provided sick leave, for:

Chart 19. (Continued)

Your Sickness and Disability Benefits

Long Term Disability Income Insurance
If after **26** weeks you remain totally and permanently disabled, you will be eligible to receive estimated monthly payments of:

$416 from the Long Term Disability Plan, until age 65.*

Lump Sum Benefits
Additional benefits for total and permanent disability:

$4,150 Your Profit Sharing Account.

Your Current Life Insurance Protection

Lump Sum Death Benefits
$20,000 Group Life Insurance.
Beneficiary: **JANE DOE**
$4,150 Your Profit Sharing Account.
Beneficiary: **JANE DOE**
$255 Social Security.
$24,405 Estimated Lump Sum Total.

Monthly Family Income Benefits
$420 Estimated monthly maximum family benefit from Social Security.

Additional Accident Death Benefits
$50,000 Accidental Death and Dismemberment occurring on or off the job.
Beneficiary: **JANE DOE**
$25,000 Accidental Death and Dismemberment for commercial air travel on Company business.
Beneficiary: **JANE DOE**

Your Life Insurance After Retirement

$15,000 Group-Life Insurance.
$255 Social Security.
$15,255 Estimated Lump Sum Total.

---

* Subject to reductions to a minimum of **$5,000 AT AGE 71**

Chart 19.   (Continued)

Your Profit Sharing Account

$3,500	Your Profit Sharing Account as of **DEC 31, 1969**
$500	Company Contributions and Forfeitures.
$150	Increase (Decrease) due to Fund Investments.
$4,150	Your Profit Sharing Account as of **DEC 31, 1970**
$48,243	Your estimated Profit Sharing Account at normal retirement.

Annual Value Added to Your Income

Benefits are provided by . . . □ Profit Sharing Plan □ Retirement Plan □ Hospital Surgical and Major Medical Plan □ Long Term Disability Plan □ Accidental Death and Dismemberment Plan □ Group Life Insurance Plan □ Vacations and Holidays □ Social Security □ Workmen's Compensation □ Unemployment Insurance.

$3,674 is the total estimated annual cost of providing these benefits for you.

$2,877 is the portion of the above annual cost which is paid for you by the Company.

$797 is the portion of the above annual cost paid by you.

For   **J. J. DOE**
As of   **JANUARY 1, 1971**
                                                                   999-99-9999   31

Group-Life Insurance.*

* Reduced by Social Security disability benefits. State disability benefits or Workmen's Compensation benefits which you may receive.

ment. Getting the employee benefit story across to employees is absolutely essential! There are undoubtedly other ways to do this; Chart 19 is one way, and an effective one.

Every employee knows what a bank statement is; this is something he can understand. This is the rationale for giving him some balance sheet and some P&L, if you wish to call it such, of his position in the industrial environment that he participates in. We give such an accounting to the corporate stockholders of our free enterprise system. We surely owe our employees no less an accounting. Who knows, but if they have the proper tools with which to assess their corporation in its multinational fight for survival and their own place in this same economic arena, they may well join with their corporation to define more effectively the path ahead for prosperity to both.

Corporations are in a constant quest for increased productivity. Up until now, it has been understandable that most employees look on such a quest with concern as if it were rooted in some form of adversary relationship. With better communication with employees as to their increasing costs to the corporate enterprise, assuming the credibility barrier can be effectively breached, it may be possible to awaken in them a growing awareness of the real need for productivity advances. If and when our employees can identify in their own minds that their future benefit cost trends can only be supported by parallel future growth trends in revenues or in improvement trends in productivity, then, and only then, will the corporate enterprise be able to effectively cope with the pressures of the rising costs of man.

CHAPTER 6

MAN AS AN "INVESTMENT"

Accountants generally think of man in terms of cost, that is, an overhead expense, a charge against operations, a committed cost only relieved by "bodies out the door." This does not apply to direct labor which is productive and hence may temporarily be deferred from the inevitable charge against income by being in the transitional stage called inventories (either work-in-process or finished goods) where a piece of man may on sufferance be permitted to be temporarily capitalized.

What kind of pseudomasochism demands that we think of man in such terms. Can not we begin to see man instead as another form of asset available to the industrial enterprise. Capital is unquestioned in its role as a necessary and fundamental asset. Until expended, capital takes its place on our balance sheets as cash, investments, or such, a symbol generally of corporate strength that augurs well for the future. Equipment is another tool of production, a necessary resource to most modern industrial enterprises. Some corporations are highly mechanized, like the modern textile mill of today where one man may tend a cluster of highly automated machines. There is never a doubt in any accountant's mind that a piece of machinery is not only a necessary resource of management, but also is a capital asset for the benefit, not merely of the present, but for a stream of future years. The accountant knows that capital assets are investments which are capitalized and reported as assets of the corporation, to be charged off as costs only pro rata over some protracted period of future time.

And what of product definition, sometimes in the form of patents, sometimes in the form of accumulated research and development expenditures, the end result of which is a set of prints and drawings on which a product is defined. Are not these considered assets of the corporation, oftentimes capitalized and reported as such on the Balance Sheet, other times not reported, for reasons of tax practice or ultraconservatism, but always assigned a value to the corporation when a merger, acquisition, or other disposition of these assets are involved.

And what of man? Is he not also a valuable and necessary tool of production, as equally important to the corporation as capital and equipment? Capital and equipment are assets certainly, but passive assets, requiring man to translate them into effective earning power. Man, therefore, is the dynamic catalyst in the equation, not only in a "direct labor" context but in every activity of the corporate enterprise in which man is involved. But, while of such crucial importance, is man, nevertheless, considered as an asset of the corporation? Never! Man is considered as an element of cost, either direct cost or indirect cost, ignominiously assigned the demeaning term "burden." Man is not an asset of the corporation, but a burden to it: hence he is reported invariably as an element of cost which terminates only in accordance with the rules of the accountant— "bodies out the door."

We have indicated that cash is an asset; a further extension of this statement is that the cost of raising a public debt issue for the corporation is generally considered an asset to be deferred on the Balance Sheet and charged off against income over the life of the debt instrument.

Similarly, installation costs, freight in, and such, associated with machinery and equipment, are considered as equally an asset and are capitalized and charged off against income over the depreciable life of the equipment. But what of man, the nonasset? Have not we discovered that it costs to recruit him, to relocate him to the job site, to orient and train him, and, lastly, to make him truly an efficient and productive resource? Until man has gone through his "pilot run" and has built up a sufficient learning curve, he has not reached his potential contribution to the corporate enterprise. Is it not valid, then, that his costs up until this point of time are really a form of investment—front-end costs to develop the asset and bring it to the point of productivity? And why are these front-end costs any different than the other examples earlier cited? It is hard to see how anyone can claim that they are different, and yet accountants continue to hold to the accounting theory that it is proper and perfectly consistent, inasmuch as we treat man as a cost, to treat the first investment in him merely as additional front-end costs. How on earth do we justify this accounting philosophy? Because it is nonmaterial? I think we have already indicated in our chapter on transience that the costs of bringing a man "on stream" are not insignificant, and if your turnover rate is appreciable and your annual expenditures for front-end investments in people are material, are you really correct in adhering to the concept that it is proper to charge such costs off as period costs? The only defense of such logic is either nonmateriality in fact, or because once the practice has been altered, the consistent recurrent use of such new accounting practice in future years would yield really the same result, so why do it?

I am afraid that accountants are often lazy and seek out too often the course of least resistance. It may be true that once the changeover has been made, the effect on annual results thereafter is much the same unless a personnel buildup occurs. But if such a personnel buildup does occur, are not we overpenalizing operations by charging off currently elements of cost which are in reality related to future period benefits? And what of our biblical slogan, "Match the expense against the revenue it creates"? This surely is a departure from our accounting bible.

So much for challenging our current concepts. These are certainly something that should be examined from the standpoint of theory. If you are a purist, it is hard to see how you can conclude that these costs are not properly deferrable front-end investments, similar to tooling costs of a new production model, and such. If you are a pragmatist, then charge them off to costs as "period expenses," which is what most of us have been doing.

But apart from theory and practicality, is not there an additional element to be considered? We have discussed merely the impact of this philosophical dialogue on earnings per share, as currently reported. Is not there something we are missing? I refer to our obligation to point the way for our managements to focus on the issues that face them in corporate decision-making, armed with the full set of facts, not an imasculated version. If investment costs of people were capitalized, would not it help to focus more clearly on the importance of proper people planning, proper hiring, better forecasting, better trade-off between "make for stock" or cost of production, and, lastly, less cost inefficiency of layoffs? When managements know they have a sizable investment in slow-moving inventories, they think first about how they can liquidate this investment for some value before they decide just to dump it and write it off. With people-costs, managements that do not see the real investment cost are robbed of this judgement factor and are more likely to "dump" people without understanding the materiality of the writeoff of asset power that they have decided on. I contend that if we allow this to happen, we have simply not done an adequate job of financial counseling.

A third factor that needs to be explored is apparent in any consideration of man as an investment. This factor relates to the decision to "buy" man in the first instance. This decision is usually made rather glibly by most managements. The job is not getting done, so you go out and hire another body. How often do we ask ourselves, "which resource is my best alternative?" Such alternatives might be as follows:

An additive to payroll roster, that is, man.
Greater use of overtime for present roster.
Use of outside subcontracting services or job shoppers.
Greater automation—invest, instead, in machinery.
Value analysis—reduce the need.

The basic question we should be asking ourselves here is, "Can we really afford man?" This may sound silly, but it is not. Man is an expensive resource when you add all his fringe benefits to his basic wage. This is why it becomes so very important to identify, to capture, and to report all these fringes so we can be sure we understand fully the real cost of man. When we understand his real cost, we can more properly evaluate him as an alternative resource and answer this question, "can we really afford man?" Furthermore, as we have pointed out, man's cost is rising rapidly. It is important to keep this trend in mind, and as man's cost trend rises, we must be continually comparing this to the similar rising cost trends of other alternative resources. Adequate attention is not given to this matter.

Perhaps the best way to approach this question is to place all alternatives on a return on investment (ROI) calculation basis. ROI computations have long been a commonplace norm for capital expenditure evaluations. But have you ever done an ROI on man? The answer is "probably not"! And why not, if man lends himself to such a calculation? Let us explore how this could be done in Chart 20.

I am afraid too often that such cost comparison of alternatives as may be made in Chart 20 is somewhat superficially done. Let us examine the alternatives:

1. *Add man to roster*—To develop a comparable cost for any useful comparative purpose, we need to know:

   (a) Man's direct cost in wages.
   (b) Man's total fringe and indirect cost.
   (c) The front-end investment in man and how short a period this might be amortized over. This involves consideration of the risk of brevity of the business need to be filled.
   (d) And what about "hind-end investment" or the residual disposition cost of man, that is, severance pay, cost to terminate, and some average unemployment compensation cost loading? This should really be added, too, and amortized over average job turnover span.

2. *Use of overtime instead*—The easiest and most expedient decision is, of course, to extend the productive workday, or work week, and resort to overtime on a regular basis. In any event, this is usually the front-end decision that is made, and if the need continues, other alternatives may well be explored as a replacement to the overtime choice. The disadvantages of overtime are that it involves a significant premium of 150% of base wage for the overtime hours worked. No one wants to pay 150% more for the labor content of his product, at least not for very long.

Chart 20. Calculation of ROI For Man

	Present Method	Hire Additional Personnel
Minimum period for program	3 years	3 years
Present cost		
Method:	Purchased from outside vendor	
Per unit	$125	
Qty.	700	
Per annum	$87,500	
Proposed cost		
Method:		Hire 3 add'l. men
Direct costs:		
3.00 per hour × 40 hours per week × 50 weeks		$6,000 per yr.
Fringes at 30%		1,800 per yr.
Total direct costs		$7,800
Indirect costs at 150%		11,700
Total costs per man		$19,500
Add'l per annum cost (3 men)		$58,500
Entrance and exit costs		
Costs to recruit 3 × $600		$1,800
Costs to train 3 × $800		2,400
Exit costs 3 × $200		600
Potential severance costs 3 × $3,000		9,000
		$13,800
Potential savings		
Present costs		$87,500
Proposed new cost per year		58,500
Savings per year		$29,000
Entrance and exit costs		$13,800
Return on investment		210%
Pay back period		Less than 6 months

An additional factor is the fatigue factor—there seems to be general agreement that at some point of time workers do become susceptible to a fatigue factor through prolonged overtime and should this occur, not only can productivity decline, but also quality can deteriorate and even safety can be jeopardized. The use of overtime should really be confined to a reasonably short-term solution to the production problem. There is also another factor—prolonged access to the higher paycheck that overtime brings to the worker usually renders him dissatisfied after his overtime is reduced and he feels that somehow he is underpaid. People do not mind working less but they rarely want to accept being paid less. I am afraid that the relationship of overtime pay to overtime hours, a variable, is more intellectually accepted than emotionally accepted.

3. *Use of outside contractors or job shoppers*—It is so much easier to go outside for the short pull, but the merits of doing so really depend on the assessment of the following factors:

   (a) How short a pull is it? If it's a longer pull, then it may well be cheaper to do it yourself.
   (b) What premium are you paying the job shopper or outside contractor? Remember, he has got the same cost as you have, that is, man and his fringes. On top of this you must compensate the outside contractor for use of his facilities and overheads, his risk, and his profit; the only potential saving offsetting this is the transience costs, "front-end" and "hind-end."
   (c) How important is control of timing, quality, and knowledge of the task? If relatively routine, chances are the outside contractor may be the best short-term bet; otherwise, you may have to do it yourself merely for better protection.
   (d) Is there any special equipment involved that you have "in house" and the outside contractor does not have and would have to procure to accommodate you? He will want to be held harmless for such a unique commitment on his part, and this could increase his real cost to you.

In spite of all these negative comments, there is a tendency to want to do everything "in house," and there is, therefore, a risk that the real usefulness of an outside contractor will not be seriously and objectively examined as an alternative. This risk should be recognized and avoided.

4. *Greater automation*—When a greater need arises, the easiest and laziest response to that need is to go out and hire another body. When people in the mainstream of the industrial treadmill are caught up in a quickened pace of coping with day-to-day transaction load, it is the point of least

resistance to make the quick decision that requires least study. But this may not be the most economic decision. It is probable that the reaction lead time to hiring another body is far less than the lead time for examining the economics of automation as a viable alternative, getting quotes for the necessary equipment, and, lastly, obtaining ultimate delivery of such equipment. Thus the odds are that the body will be hired as a short-term response to the need, and then, if management is alert enough, the attractiveness of further automation will be studied as a means of reducing cost once the job is in progess and the need is being met: "Satisfy the need first; worry about cost second." This is certainly the pragmatic outlook of our industrial managers, but it is not necessarily an efficient approach and surely involves a heavy penalty for poor advance planning. ROI calculations in support of equipment purchase justification are familiar to accountants so there is no need to belabor the calculation here; the only point of interest is that this is, nevertheless, a definite and serious alternative to the decision on whether to "buy man" at any point of time.

5. *Value Analysis*—When greater need for man arises, as it does repeatedly, there is the very real choice between responding to the demands of the occasion or of studying ways of reducing the need itself. Our general and overwhelming tendency is to do the former: that is, to go out and hire man. In the garden of industrial growth, there is a strong psychological focus on building and adding to the structure of the present organism. Pruning away the jungle of excessive past growth, or of obsolete and archaic activities, reports, procedures, and such, is an unpopular, unexciting activity. Therefore, it is given low priority attention at best or ignored at worst. It is more natural for managers to want to place in motion new plans, new programs, and new ideas that capture their enthusiasm and imagination, than to turn their attention inward to self-examination and determination of what is no longer needed and what can be pruned away. This is contrary to human nature. And yet, we all recognize intellectually that man can not live in a jungle—what is excessive must be pruned away for the health of the organism. Therefore, value analysis, otherwise known as reducing product costs, possibly which might involve reducing the need for man himself, is yet another necessary alternative to be considered.

No examination of the comparative merits of buying man or selecting some other alternative can be undertaken without understanding what man's true costs are. Even given a fairly reliable accounting of man's fringes, it can be seen from the following summary that the wrong choice could still be made if we were not to include also the concept of man as an investment, an investment

Chart 21. Alternative Investment Choices for 20% Increase in Demand

	Present Cost ($)	Alternative 1 Overtime for Additional Demand ($)	Alternative 2 Hire Two Additional People ($)	Alternative 3 Use Outside Subcontractors ($)
Department direct labor				
10 Persons at 3.00 per hour × 40 hours per week × 50 weeks	60,000	78,000	72,000	
Fringes at 30%	18,000	23,400	21,600	
Indirect department costs	90,000	90,000	90,000	219,000
Per Year	168,000	191,400	183,600	219,000
Entrance and exit costs				
2 × $600, recruitment costs		0	1,200	0
2 × $800, costs to train		0	1,600	0
2 × $200, exit costs		0	400	0
2 × $3,000, possible severance costs		0	6,000	0
		191,400	192,800	219,000

NOTE. Alternative 2 presumes that the increased demand need will remain for 12 months or more. If it is less, this choice obviously becomes less attractive.

which must be amortized over his useful contribution to the corporation (see Chart 21).

It must be concluded, therefore, that by our failure to account properly for man in terms that parallel our recognition of other assets of the corporation, accountants are no doubt misleading managements down many a false trail to incorrect and improper decision-making—decision-making that may be leading to adverse economic consequences for the industrial corporation.

CHAPTER 7

PENSION FUNDS:
THE IMPORTANCE OF
FUND PERFORMANCE

In an earlier chapter we indicated that one of the most dynamic elements in the cost of pension benefits to the corporation was the performance of its Pension Fund investment vehicle over a period of years. This variable is of such significance to the financial executive that it is important enough to be the subject matter of a separate chapter.

OBJECTIVE OF THE PENSION TRUST PORTFOLIO

It first seems appropriate to define the basic objective of the pension investment portfolio. The rationale of the Pension Trust in the first instance is that the corporation makes dollar contributions on a regular basis to a separate vehicle, distinct in its responsibilities and free from access from the corporation fathering these same contributions. And why is this so? The rationale is that if such sums are allowed to remain in the corporate domain, comingled with general corporate funds, when need arises, the corporate hands may willingly or unwillingly reach into the till. The risk is ever present that these sacred funds may be used for general corporate purposes with closer urgencies than that of some future retirement benefit for employees. This "immoral" prospect has long since been removed from temptation, and corporations may not obtain a tax deduction for pension contributions unless such contributions are irrevocably placed beyond the control of the corporation itself, and thus the need for a pension investment vehicle.

These vehicles may take a variety of forms, for example, insurance contracts, bank trust agreements, or trust agreements administered privately. These are the usual choices, and while each possesses optimum characteristics for the needs of an individual situation, I have long favored a bank trusteed form of plan over an insured plan because of the opportunity to minimize company cost through fund performance.

Getting back to objectives, the objective of a pension trust is obviously to receive funds from the corporation for the benefit of future pension payments of eligible corporate employees under the terms of the approved Pension Plan. Because of the serious fiduciary nature of this mandate, it has over the years been the fundamental objective of all Pension Trusts to preserve the principal of the portfolio to the utmost ability of the trustee, often to the sacrifice of optimum annual earning power of the trust and certainly of market appreciation of the trust. Such considerations were entirely secondary to the fundamental need to make payment to the retiree when called on to do so. As a consequence, over the years, it is not strange to find that trusteed plan experience has been characterized by considerable conservatism, to the point of excess in the opinion of many. Performance is a relatively modern concept, one that over the years has been beneath the dignity certainly of many prominent banking institutions' pension trust departments.

I believe this objective is undergoing a change in today's performance oriented investment world. Competitive pressures of the institutional community could not continue to be ignored even by our prominent banks. Big city banks are certainly more aware of the needs of modern day pension trusts and are often quite aggressive in pursuing such needs to the extent they are compatible with their institutional image for integrity, basic reliability, and professionalism.

One should not conclude that the Pension Trust objective of being able to liquidate the pension commitment when due is in any way altered in today's modern world. Our pension trustees are far from a bunch of "swingers" with employee funds. Rather, it is recognized that pension plans have generally less need for short-term liquidity than they have for longer term sound performance under reasonable investment principles to protect against the inflationary spirals that continually threaten all pension plans.

HOW DOES A PENSION TRUST WORK

It is common practice, when a pension plan has been set into motion, to have a professional actuarial firm annually assess the roster of eligible employees covered by the plan in light of the terms of the plan itself. Out of this study comes an actuarial calculation that determines the contribution that the corporation should make into the trust, in light of the agreed on actuarial assumptions, to render the trust sound for its future purposes at this point of time, usually the fiscal year end of the corporation. Acting on this professional report, the corporation makes its cash contribution into the trust. At this point such funds have reached the point of no return to the corporation itself, and they are held in trust for the benefit of the covered employees themselves. But this does not mean that the corporation has no further continuing interest in such funds, nor does it imply that the trustee does not recognize the corporation's continuing interest in such funds, subject to the proper discharge by the trustee of its fiduciary obligation to the corporation's employees. In the usual form of pension plan, the plan defines the dollar benefit to be paid to the retiring employee. This is an obligation of the plan, and it exists without regard to the successful or unsuccessful investment performance of the trust itself. This risk resides entirely with the corporation. Being aware of this, the trustee does, therefore, feel a sense

Chart 22.   Effect of Increasing Interest Rate on the Annual Cost to Provide a Pension of $10,000 at Age 65 to an Employee Now Age 30

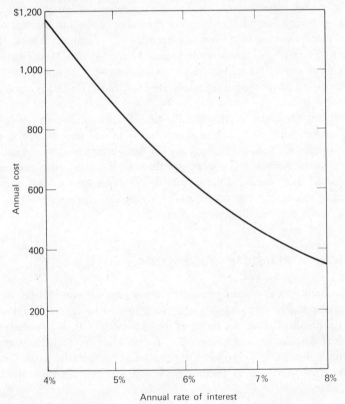

Annual rate of interest

Chart 23.   Effect of Increasing Fund Performance on Pre-Tax Annual Pension Cost and Earnings per share After-Taxes [Given: Base annual pretax pension cost is $675,000. When pension fund performance earns 4% annually (yield), 2,500,000 shares are outstanding, or 13.5 ¢ per share cost.

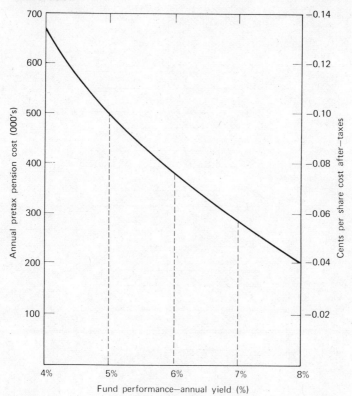

of responsibility to the corporation to assist, insofar as prudent performance will allow, in holding to a minimum the cost of pension benefits to the corporation. This can be achieved by fund performance.

Chart 22 demonstrates the dramatic effect of an improvement of fund performance on pension costs.

If we extrapolate the data in Chart 22 into its potential impact on our model corporation, XYZ, then we can observe the results shown in Chart 23.

It is quite apparent from the hypothetical illustration in Chart 23 that fund performance does in fact exercise a powerful influence over pension costs to the corporation. I qualify this by stating that it is only true over the long term. Cer-

Chart 24. An Example of Variations of Fund Performance in Terms of Growth of Portfolio of Specific Corporation "A" (March 1, 1954 through December 31, 1965)

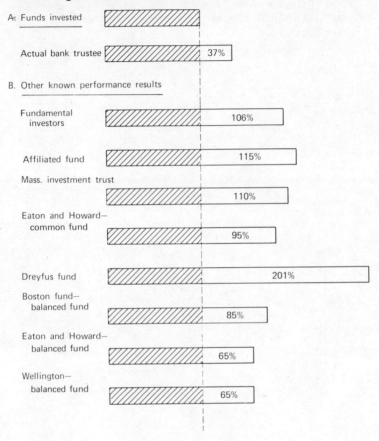

A: Funds invested

Actual bank trustee — 37%

B. Other known performance results

Fundamental investors — 106%

Affiliated fund — 115%

Mass. investment trust — 110%

Eaton and Howard— common fund — 95%

Dreyfus fund — 201%

Boston fund— balanced fund — 85%

Eaton and Howard— balanced fund — 65%

Wellington— balanced fund — 65%

tainly short-term performance, favorable or adverse, would not be recognized as a valid actuarial assumption or a valid change in actuarial assumptions already selected. We have also earlier referred to Accounting Practice Bulletin 8, which requires that the economic impact of changes in actuarial assumptions of this sort be spread over a period of years rather than realized as an immediate reprieve of cost reduction in the year of changeover.

But the illustration discussed is a hypothesis; what about the "real world"? Do such disparities of fund performance in fact challenge pension funds? The answer is an emphatic "yes"! This can be best illustrated by an actual study I made of the historic performance of the Pension Trust of a company of which I was Chief Financial Officer. My study centered around taking the actual pension trust performance of our pension trustee, a major metropolitan bank, over a span of 10 years. In making the comparisons with this performance and the historic performance of a number of the more popular, and responsible, larger mutual funds, I had the dollars and timing of cash receipts of funds by the trust, as well as cash disbursements by the trust, applied intact to each of the other alternative funds. The results were rather startling (see Chart 24).

The exhibit in Chart 24 should be examined in light of the observation that the pension plan was to provide a fixed dollar benefit to employees on retirement; therefore, the entire advantage of fund performance accrued to the sole benefit of the corporation and not to the employee. In this illustration, by selecting any other of the chosen alternatives, the pension costs to the company could have been *reduced in all instances*, anywhere from $198,000 to $1,175,000, a rather significant spread of possible alternatives and even given the 10 year time span, certainly a significant enough reduction in per annum

Chart 25. Standard and Poor's Composite 500 Stock Index 1965–1971 (value of $10,000 invested 1/1/65, including reinvested dividends)

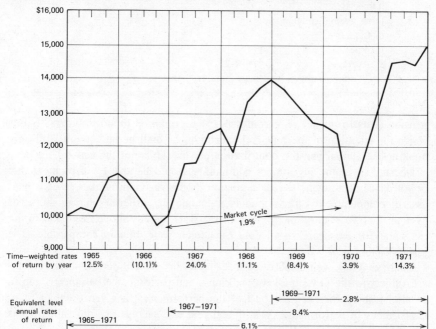

Chart 26.   Mutual Funds *

	6 Months 1973	Year 1972	5½ Years 1968 to 6/30/73	10½ Years 1963 to 6/30/73	Return
I. *Growth funds*					
A. Large Growth Funds (1972 Year-End Assets Over $300,000,000) Averages	−22.0	+15.0	+1.7	+157.5	1.1%
B. Other Growth Funds					
1. (Objective: Maximum Capital Gain) Averages	−28.7	+10.1	−16.8	−93.1	0.7%
2. (Objective: Long Term Growth of Capital & Income) Averages	−21.2	+13.4	+3.0	+107.1	1.2%

pension costs to impact on earnings per share reported to stockholders. Is this worth the attention of the financial executive, or shall he be content with only booking the annual pension contribution per the advice of the actuary?

No student of the investment community would believe for a moment that performance of a given 10-year segment of the investment market place is necessarily comparable to other segments of the market, earlier or later, of shorter or even up to 10 years duration, for that matter. But the study above was made during the same 10-year span, so all data considered were directly comparable. The results cannot be discounted.

I believe it is a well-established fact that all investment performance vehicles are subject to the same market conditions, and performance parameters run in parallel fashion for even the best of the performers at a given point of time. Consistency of performance, year in and year out, seems to be most illusive, as Chart 25 of Standard & Poor's composite 500 stock index shows.

Chart 26.   (Continued)

	6 Months 1973	Year 1972	5½ Years 1968 to 6/30/73	10½ Years 1963 to 6/30/73	Return
II. *Other diversified common stock funds*					
A. Objective: Growth & Current Income Averages	−15.6	+12.1	+11.5	+98.9	2.6%
B. Objective: Growth & Current Income with Relative Stability Averages	−16.1	+11.6	+14.5	+100.7	3.4%
III. *Balanced funds* Averages	−11.6	+11.6	+17.3	+77.8	3.8%
IV. *Income funds* Averages	−9.1	+7.6	+18.6	+93.5	5.6%
Bond funds Averages	−2.6	+8.3	+24.8	+50.8	6.9%

* Approximate percentage change in net assets per share with capital gains (reinvested) and income dividends added back.

Looking at Chart 25, how does one determine what is a fair and relatively riskless fund return to use for actuarial projections, 2.8, 8.4, or 6.1%? This question makes a big difference on the cost of the pension plan as we have seen from previous charts.

Probably the best illustration of comparative fund performance over any meaningful period of time can be found in the published reports of Wiesenberger. These reports indicate the dimensions (condensed) in Chart 26 to the comparative alternative.

If I have established that the fund performance is a most versatile and dynamic factor, what then does the financial executive do to optimize his economics to the extent that market conditions will allow?

There is no substitute for vigilance and involvement on a regular basis with the Pension Fund Trustee. Quarterly reports of fund performance, quarterly comparisons with how general market conditions are doing, perhaps quarterly or semiannual conferences with the fund manager of the pension trust to discuss performance, views of economic outlook, fund needs and strategies all are definitely important and constitute a role for the financial executive that he would be foolish to ignore or defer as secondary in his priority scale of importance.

From time to time it may also be of value to have an objective and independent critique of fund performance made by one of the larger investment houses. In my experience, they are more than willing to perform this service if you will reciprocate by assuring them that they will, in turn, receive a share of pension fund placement business directed their way. It is a "you scratch my back; I'll scratch yours" concept. Since, as with compensating balances versus bank working funds, someone is going to get the investment placement business, why pass up a legitimate opportunity to get some value received for the corporation's benefit for it?

If you are reluctant to bargain for a "free service," then there are a variety of professional consultants who, for a fee, will "audit" your pension fund performance objectively and render recommendations. Because these firms are not in a position to receive commission business as a result of their recommendations, their advice is presumed to be more objective than is the former "free service."

One further route for the financial executive to follow is to inject the element of competition into the pension fund itself. This can be achieved by dividing the fund in two or more parts and assigning each part to a different unrelated fund manager. Each fund manager obviously knows that he is competing against other fund managers; hence he should give the matter of performance of your trust closer attention than he might possibly do otherwise. Fund managers like to eat like the rest of us, and this practice of fund division has become more common in recent years. It used to be "unprofessional" to suggest such a prospect but not so these days; there is too much at stake to worry about the Marquis of Queensbury rules.

The question might be asked, "How does one go about selecting a fund manager?" I am not sure there is any set protocol for doing this other than one prescribed by good judgment. Assuming the decision has been made to use a bank-trusteed plan rather than an insured plan, the financial executive would consult with his presently established financial community contacts to discuss the subject. Actually, he will not have to take the initiative; they and hordes of others will have anticipated this need long before and will have deluged him with solicitations. He will have more of a problem fighting off competing contenders than identifying prospects. As with most negotiators, you will want to review the past track record of each candidate in terms of performance, perhaps even checking with your counterpart in other clients they are now serving, to see how he feels about the quality of their relationship with the Trust Department of the bank.

You will certainly want to review the ability of the bank to render the services you require and define the logistics of administrative details and such. Fees, of course, enter the discussion, and you should have a good idea in advance of the entire projected financial cost of your relationship with the bank in handling your pension plan. Certainly there will be variations between financial institutions and fund managers in the peripheral services other than the fund performance itself that can be discussed, and to the extent these services are important to you, this may affect your selection. Your biggest problem may be possible conflict between the financial relationships you or your company may now have and your true and impartial selection of the proper institution to serve as fund manager. It is a little difficult sometimes not to give your pension fund management to the financial institution that has a representative serving on your Board of Directors. Sometimes this may be a satisfactory choice; at other times, not. Personally, I have always felt that it was not a good practice to have members of financial institutions serving on your Board of Directors because it does present potential conflict of interest risks that are not desirable. The method of selecting a fund manager is to shop around for one in a highly competitive market place. Never doubt, they all want your business.

I think that it is important to point out, however, that the selection of a bank to serve as pension plan trustee and to manage the trust is not necessarily synonymous with the selection of a fund manager. The fund manager may well be the Pension Trust Department of that same bank, and, frequently, this is the case. But it is often the case that the fund manager may be an investment banking or counseling firm, with the bank trustee merely serving as the custodian vehicle for holding the assets of the fund and administering the receipts and disbursements of the fund. Sometimes the fund manager is in reality a committee of the corporation's own executives who retain professional advice from a variety of sources outside the company and, again, use the bank trustee merely in a custodial capacity. Often, one or more mutual funds, selected perhaps from the information published by the Wiesenberger Report, will in reality be the fund manager. All of these combinations can and do happen in the world of the pension trust. The choice is yours. Performance can be fairly readily measured and, to an ever-increasing degree these days, it can be compared with performance data of other funds, published from a variety of sources, all of which are accessible. If, after a reasonable period of time, you are dissatisfied with the performance of your fund in general comparison with the world at large, there is no real deterrent to changing fund managers. This happens frequently these days, but even so, this flexibility should not be allowed to invite capriciousness on the part of the corporation.

One note of caution on the subject of fund performance should be sounded. It is all well and good to be aware of the impact of fund performance on company costs, and it is certainly the financial executive's job to try to achieve over the long pull an average or better-than-average yield, but beyond this the temptation to maximize fund performance too aggressively is to court danger. This subject received excellent attention in the February 11, 1974 issue of *Pensions and Investments,* where Steven C. Lenthold and Walter H. May, Jr. point out the following:

Most investment managers have a 'battle plan' they tend to stick with through all seasons. The in-built performance-record trap is obvious. A manager's performance naturally tends to crest along with the popularity of the types of stocks in which he specializes.

Performance watchers, attracted by rising performance, too often buy in at the peak of a style's popularity cycle.

This point is ably illustrated by a chart in this article (Chart 27).

Before leaving the subject of fund performance, I would like to touch on its impact on the employee. We have discussed how fund performance affects the costs to the corporation, but what about the employee himself?

In a conventional pension plan, the employee who stays to retirement is not impacted at all by the interim fund fluctuations. His pension benefit is defined by the terms of the plan ifself, and he is thereby shielded from the risk of portfolio experience. (He is also shielded from the potential benefit of portfolio performance as well.) But if his pension benefit is being provided through the

**Chart 27.   Annual Performance Ranking of Two
Popular Mutual Funds among 39,
1951 through 1960**

	Keystone S-4 Aggressive Growth Style	Chemical Fund Moderate Growth Style
1951	29	1
1952	1	39
1953	38	14
1954	5	27
1955	3	3
1956	8	33
1957	35	1
1958	1	27
1959	1	4
1960	36	23

vehicle of a deferred profit sharing trust, which is common, the answer is different. Yes, he is affected by fund performance. If he happens to terminate in a temporary market downturn, his shares of the profit sharing/pension trust are valued at that time and at that level of market value, and they are removed from the trust and either segregated for his account for future installment payouts or paid out to him in cash lump sum. In either event, he is forced to "sell out" at the market in accordance with the provisions of the plan. If you refer back to Chart 25, it should be clear that if this performance trend line were that of the specific pension/profit sharing trust covering employee John Jones, his payout would be adversely affected if he were terminated involuntarily in the summer of 1970 as opposed to termination either in the summer of 1969 or in 1971. Of course, if John Jones took his payout in cash lump sum and turned around and invested it back in the market, he could recoup his position, perhaps even in similar manner to the improvement in Chart 25 from 1970 to 1971. But the likelihood of this happening is not great. If John Jones is retiring, his segregated funds will undoubtedly be invested in stocks that protect principal and yield income rather than invested in inflation hedged common stocks. Or, if John Jones gets a smaller lump sum distribution and invests it in a business, a home or such, there is no doubt he has less dollars available to him to spend in this manner via his termination from the plan in the summer of 1970. This is one of the unfortunate aspects of fund performance where a fixed retirement income guaranty is not present. Employees who remain with the fund ride out market fluctuations; employees who are forced out of the plan in a slump get hurt. In Chapter 12, I deal specifically with a suggestion on how to correct this unfortunate problem.

CHAPTER 8

INCREASED LONGEVITY

Previous chapters have dealt with the cost to a corporate enterprise of providing during the productive years of the working man for his postproductive income after retirement from the company. We have also dealt with the problem of how this cost is now being increased because the period of productive employment is shortened through the additional factor of obsolescence. There remains yet another factor in this economic jigsaw puzzle, and this factor relates to the increasing longevity of the life cycle of modern man. It is a well-published fact that the average life expectancy of working males has been steadily and persistently increasing because of the advances of modern medical technology. We seem successfully pushing the threshold of death further and further away. This seems to be a tremendous triumph to our social and humanitarian environment and yet is this really true, or is it a mixed blessing of sorts? Working man is living longer. At the same time, retirement ages, once 70, then 65, are now moving toward the mark of 60. In addition, as we have observed, depreciation of man, marked by a shorter productive life, is additionally exaggerated by the impact of obsolescence as well. This is happening at the same time as the working man himself is enjoying longer active physical life. His productive industrial life is shrinking while his physical life span is expanding. Surely this remarkable phenomenon has tremendous, and perhaps as yet largely unrecognized, consequences for the future, not only for the social planners of tomorrow but also, in the immediate perspective of this book, for the financial executive as well.

This chapter poses this issue directly before the financial executive, for he may, in all likelihood, have to provide an economic solution to tomorrow's longer living working man and charge such costs over a steadily shortening period of productive utility. Undoubtedly, this fact has major cost implications that the financial executive will have to face and find proper cost accounting solutions for in tomorrow's world. Let us examine these concepts in more detail.

We have already indicated in a previous chapter that the life expectancy of an employee is a key variable in the determination of pension costs. We have also alluded to the fact that man is living longer in this world of increasing death control. Over the years, this fact has expressed itself in various publications in different press media, so that it is well accepted. In pension actuarial calculations, this same development has reflected itself into what are referred to as "Mortality Tables." These tables are in common use throughout the actuarial profession, and they take two forms. The first table relates to the average life expectancy of employees who have in fact "made it" to age 65, and who may be expected to actually receive pension benefits. Chart 28 shows the mortality tables historical trend.

Chart 28. Mortality Tables of Life Expectancy of Person Reaching Age 65

Title of Table	Year Table Published	Average Life Expectancy at 65, in years	
		Males	Females
Combined annuity	1928	12.7	15.2
1937 standard annuity	1938	14.4	17.6
GA 1951	1951	14.2	17.7
GA 1971	1971	15.1	19.2

In simplest terms, Chart 28 means that for a retired employee who is to be paid a $10,000 per annum pension for life, in 1971 his pension trust would expect to pay out to him $9,000 more than they would have expected for a comparable benefit to the same man 20 years early. Similarly, in 1971 they would expect to pay $25,000 more in pension payouts to the same man for the same benefit than they would have expected to 40 years earlier. The benefit has not changed in this instance, nor has the man; he just is living longer these days; hence more benefit must be provided, which, in turn, means more cost to the pension plan, and to the corporation providing the benefit. With females the trend is even greater, which may perhaps even be more significant if we consider that it is probably increasingly more common practice these days for women to choose to remain with an industrial corporate career to retirement than it was 50 years ago. We accountants think often of "product mix," but are we as alert to "employee mix"? It is becoming more significant and will undoubtedly deserve even more attention in the future.

Our second illustration relates to death prior to retirement. As commented on earlier, it was much more common in prior years for employees to work for their entire life cycles for the corporate enterprise and just not "make it" to retirement and the golden pot of pension benefits. Chart 29, again used by the actuarial profession, shows that the likelihood of this happening has almost been cut in half, both for males as well as for females.

Recalling my earlier comments on the importance of this phenomenon on pension fund costs, you should remember that people who terminate and go to work for another company, or who die, more often than not leave behind them some contribution for pension benefits that now they will never receive. These are now called forfeitures and are reallocated to other future contributions for remaining eligible members of the pension plan. The company, of course, gains in this process by receiving credit for such forfeitures against the require-

Chart 29. Mortality Tables of Life Expectancy of Persons Prior to Reaching Age 65

	For Ages Shown, % Mortality Before 65	
Title of Table	Age 25 (%)	Age 45 (%)
Combined annuity	33.1	28.3
1937 standard annuity	30.9	26.3
GA 1951	22.1	19.7
GA 1971	18.8	16.7

ment for providing pensions for present and future employees. This business of longevity has disturbed this neat windfall and applies pressure on increased costs for the trends of pension costs.

Let us look at this problem a little more specifically. Chart 30 assumes that the pension benefit for a retired employee will start at age 60. It shows how much the pension benefit will cost at varying life expectancies of this employee.

It is startling to observe that if this employee lives to age 80 his aggregate pension payments will be almost *triple* what they would be if he only lives to age 65—this cost differential must be borne by the company, and while it is true that the actuarial averages show that living to age 80 is not yet the norm, it does not take much imagination for any financial executive to realize that we are moving in this direction. And as we so move, so will our pension costs.

Poor old XYZ company! And what is to be done about this problem? Surely we are not about to reverse the trends of the Death Control Culture. Can anyone seriously doubt that we are reentering the age of Methuselah? It is far too cavalier for accountants to scoff and disclaim any serious interest in this prospect. But if pension benefits triple from life expectancy changes from age 60 to

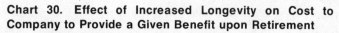

Chart 30. Effect of Increased Longevity on Cost to Company to Provide a Given Benefit upon Retirement

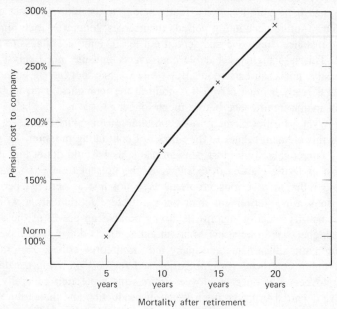

Mortality after retirement

80, is it not obvious that further geometric changes will occur if Methuselah lives in large numbers to age 80 and even beyond? And where is the financial executive in all this? Is he recording as current expense the actuarial reports for current years contributions into the pension trust, or is there some more dynamic role that he should be considering here?

There is a further question that should be asked at this point: Granted that present employees will be living longer, and hence their larger pension benefits will constitute a greater cost upon the corporation, should this cost properly be an increased charge against present earnings during the productive life of the employee himself, or should such increased costs be properly charged against future years as longevity itself occurs? A most interesting question! How does the traditional accounting axiom of "match the expense with the revenue" serve us in this instance? Any possible revenue effect of man must surely be roughly parallel to his active working cycle itself. This would argue that his retirement expenses, even his increasing expenses due to longevity, are really additional "off balance sheet" expenses that we, through hindsight, subsequently identify and throw back into prior year costs to match the true costs of man against the revenues toward which he contributed. This would seem the conventionally proper approach, surely, but is it really appropriate? Or do the costs of the future, that is, inflation, rising wage rates, rising market values of portfolio, and increasing longevity, really belong to the future and are properly chargeable to future accounting periods themselves, long after man himself, in a specific instance, has gone and served out his revenue usefulness to the corporation. This is a highly debatable controversy and one not likely to be resolved easily, nor at an early date. But while we may not have a generally accepted APB ready to dust off on this point at the moment, never doubt that it will be of major significance before much longer.

There is yet a further element to the problem of longevity that needs discussion, and this element relates to the impact of continuing inflation. As yet, this is largely unrecognized by most pension plans, as I would doubt that there are many cost of living clauses in existence at the present time. And yet, is not continuing inflation a serious problem? Is it not just as serious, perhaps far more serious, *after* retirement than before. Before retirement, a worker has some means of protection against declining purchasing power of the dollar by virtue of higher wage increases. Many union contracts do, in fact, have cost of living automatic adjustments and many industrial corporations, even in the absence of union contracts, recognize the need for cost of living escalators for their employees. But once employees retire, this protection generally ceases. They have departed from the mainstream of production and their future income now becomes the province of the Pension Plan. But inflation does not stop. Retirees, therefore, now enter the world of the fixed monthly income for the balance of their lives. Although Social Security has been and will continue to be adjusted upwards, giving some relief, what about the benefit provided in the private sector? The corporation and the employee himself, when he was productive, thought this would be adequate for the postretirement needs, but they did not count on the insidious erosion of inflation. The result is that the retiree, with each passing year, sees his once adequate pension benefit shrink in terms of what it will buy for him in each passing year's market place. The problems of the aged living on fixed incomes in today's inflationary staircase are well known; they are certainly not new. They have been chronicled in many a news media article, and they have given rise to political response in the public sector, but as yet no significant response in the private sector itself.

With longevity tables of one or two decades ago, this problem may not have been considered acute, but surely, with the increased and even accelerating longevity trends we now face, this problem cannot be long ignored. And what is the answer? The answer can only lie in providing cost of living escalator clauses into private sector retirement plans.

What financial executive or industrial relations executive is there that has not recently had a call from some company retiree who has asked if the company plans to do anything for its servants of yesteryear? And yet, if the costs of increased longevity on pension costs are already significant, what impact do you suppose a cost of living escalator clause would have on these same costs? The answer is "horrendous." The upward cost curve would surely become geometric, with the sharp slope of the curve determined only by the magnitude of estimated future inflation.

This topic is not futuristic; it is here and now. Companies and unions are in fact discussing it now. In the February 25, 1974 issue of *Pensions and Investments Magazine,* there is an article that cites that "Aluminum firms say they won't fund cost-of-living . . . the cost of funded pension plan improvement, *excluding* the unfunded cost of living increases, could easily increase fund costs . . . by double or triple the present rates within 10 years and quite probably even sooner." This article is pointing out that just providing the cost of living escalator costs on a "pay-as-you-go basis" represents in itself such an enormous pension cost increase that attempting to fund it in advance is simply out of the question.

Similarly, the February 11, 1974 issue of the same magazine reports that Kimberly-Clark Corp. increased pension benefits retroactively for retired employees and adds the following:

The boost in pension benefit payments to employees already on retirement will help them keep pace with rising living costs. . . . It's the second such increase in the past three years and will mean about $700,000 in the first year for retirees now drawing benefits. The company plans to fund additional costs by paying $500,000 annually over the next 25 years.

This is by no means the start of the parade, and other companies have been and are even now facing up to this problem. I have no doubt that more will follow this trail and that the cost increases that this dialogue points out will be on us and real indeed. Tomorrow's inflation cost to employees after retirement *will* be an additional burden to the corporation, and the phenomenon of increased longevity of such employees will define this as a *major* burden rather than merely as a burden.

CHAPTER 9

CAN WE AFFORD TO LET
EMPLOYEES RETIRE?

In the work-ethic industrial society, the respite of retirement holds an almost sacred place as the ultimate objective, cherished along the way by man, sustaining him throughout all his labors. From early times, it was extremely doubtful that many men would achieve this goal, for which, even knowing this, all nevertheless schemed and yearned. As years rolled on and technological progress brought the gradual fruits of death control, man, to an increasing extent, has in fact been "making it" in ever larger numbers. Admittedly, some are finding that it is not all it is cracked up to be when they finally reach the objective, but that is another subject. More recently yet, we find a further increasing trend toward even earlier retirement. The affluent society is assisting in this process and creating the economic environment which is making this possible on a broader scale. At the same time, we now discover that Death Control has increased longevity as a corollary, with a consequent result that the financing of retirement itself is becoming increasingly more expensive. Inflationary trend of cost of living is, of course, an additional and equally significant factor in raising the ante of retirement. Perhaps a generation ago, the attitude might have been that these increased costs were unfortunate but the burden remained, nevertheless, on the retiree himself. If he could not afford to retire, let him remain in the productive mainstream. This philosophy is disappearing, I believe, as a casualty of the onwards and upwards society. If the psychological trend is that man retires between 60 and 65 and the cost of doing so becomes higher and might discourage this practice, the consequence is not to reverse the trend of earlier retirement ot keep pace with its costs; the trend is to pass this increased cost on to the corporate enterprise itself. Let us examine some specific economics to put this dilemma in perspective.

First, let us see what pension benefits must be accumulated for a man who will retire at age 65 and who will live for five years beyond retirement. Then, let us compare this with the same pension benefits for a man who will retire at

60 but still live until age 70, that is, 10 years past retirement. Lastly, let us look at the man who will retire early at age 60 but live even longer, that is, to age 75+ (see Chart 31).

Look at the difference between these extremes in cost. Can the financial executive afford to ignore this? And what if the same phenomenon is multiplied by a payroll roster of 500, of 1000, of 10,000 persons? This is a pertinent financial problem, but is it really getting that much attention by our financial men at this time? Probably not; they are too busy turning out historic financials of elaborate format, full of debits and credits. Tomorrow's economic trends are far removed from the green eyeshade world.

But, putting this illustration aside for the moment, let us ask ourselves a very important question. "If these trends really face the modern corporate enterprise, what can be done about it?" The obvious answer to this dialogue is, "Can we really afford to let employees retire?" Is not a shorter productive life cycle for man a turn inward toward a basic inefficiency that is hostile to the financial environment of the modern industrial enterprise? Reminding ourselves again of the concept of man as a corporate asset rather than merely an expense, can we really afford economically to limit our use of man to too short a productive life? Can we afford to run any capital intensive investment, be it hospital, college, automated utility, and such over a relatively short period of time? All capital assets have a period of utility measured in hours that create the mini-

Chart 31. Comparative Effect of Retirement Age and Mortality on Pension Cost to Provide the Same Benefit upon Retirement

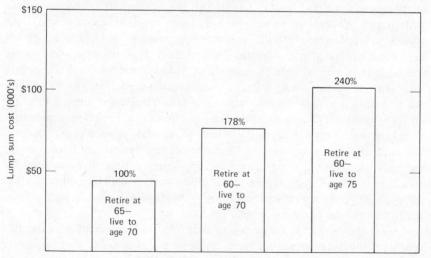

mum economics that would justify the investment itself. If a die casting machine can not be utilized roughly 75% of each shift, for three shifts around the clock, its investment is probably not justified. It is a well-recognized fact that hospitals and colleges, both highly capital intensive, cannot yet be reduced to an economically sound basis. And what about man, the asset? Is it not reasonable to believe that as the price tag for man himself goes up, whether through inflation itself or through socioeconomic progression, there may well be a minimum period of time over which these direct and indirect costs of man must be spread to make economic sense. It is hard to conceive that these pyramiding costs can be logically spread over even shorter periods of productive life and still be competitive. I doubt that man's productivity is accelerating to such a degree as to permit this. If not, then earlier retirement cannot really make economic sense in the corporate economic environment. Forgetting obsolescence and its demands for fresh talent and energy, even obsolete man surely has some economic contribution to be made to the industrial enterprise over which to spread his minimum life cycle costs to the corporation.

There is an almost axiomatic belief in our socioeconomic environment that wages have only one possible life cycle direction, that is, upward. This reflects the psychology of the "onward and upward" culture that we are in. The only possible allowable variable is the actual upward rate of wage progression itself. Of course, in pension planning, the actuarial assumption selected relating to the average annual wage rate growth factor is a critical factor in determining pension costs. This point has already been brought out in an earlier chapter.

Any financial executive who has dealt with pension planning to the extent of reviewing the results of professional actuarial studies is already aware of the startling effect that such studies reveal. This is simply illustrated by projections that today's 30-year-old factory floor sweeper presently earning $4000 per annum will be earning $14,000 per annum at point of retirement at age 65; hence the retirement pay provided for him throughout his productive career must equate to a reasonable relationship of $14,000, not $4000. This is not a little startling to the young financial executive who, confronted with this for the first time, naturally demonstrates some reluctance to go running in to his company president claiming that the floor sweeper has to have a pension benefit of at least double his present salary to have an adequate pension plan. The natural result would be stony stares at the never-ceasing absurdity of bean-counters and their ilk. Must a wage always go up, hitting a peak at retirement? Or should an industrial wage and the career of the working man himself have a full life cycle involving not only a rise but also a subsequent decline, in similar fashion to the demand curve for another product?

If we take a product in the corporate sales line, we know in advance that this product will have a certain life cycle. Its demand will probably start off slowly as recognition of the product's merits becomes more widely known and accepted. Once this happens, an expanding demand creates a bulge in the demand curve that should spell optimum economic return to the corporate enterprise. When this curve peaks and starts to decline, which it ultimately must, either through saturation, eventual infiltration of competitive products, or even market fatigue itself, the product's economic usefulness declines rapidly. And what does the corporate marketeer do in the face of such an event? Does he abandon the product, or does he try to squeeze the last incremental economics from it by downgrading the product either through discounting, lowering its sales price directly, wheeling and dealing, and such—literally a whole variety of tricks to continue to realize value for an asset that admittedly is yielding declining returns to the corporation. Probably these marketing variations are somehow related not only to an assessment of the remaining market interest in the product itself but also to the corporation's remaining inventory or tooling investment, if any, on the corporate books, that must either be recovered through additional marginal revenues or else written off against revenues of other products.

And what about man? Does he not also have a residual investment at theoretic retirement date that the corporation likewise must recover against further contribution on his part or else "write off" as an expense against the current contribution of his associates? This is obviously so, but in our concern about an orderly and disciplined logistical structure, that is, mandatory retirement at a given age, we overlook the fact that adherence to this discipline is forcing us into ever increasingly uneconomic circumstances. And for what purpose, really? To make way for younger, aggressive, and imaginative talent? Then well and good! (Not from a socioethic standpoint but probably alright from a personnel standpoint.) But other than this, because we feel that such persons have no further economic usefulness to the corporation? Nonsense! This cannot be so, nor can we be so unimaginative as to allow ourselves the luxury of this rationalization. Bear in mind I am not talking about *voluntary* retirement—this should always be provided and encouraged. I am considering only the involuntary form that says, in effect if not in so many words, "from today onward you have *nothing* to contribute to the corporate entity."

This is just not true, nor is it economically sound. Moreover, it is becoming less economically sound as the years progress. Contrary to recognizing this fact, we tend to think that an ever reducing retirement age is some great fringe benefit that only the more enlightened corporations have so far recognized.

We have already demonstrated that this thesis holds adverse economic consequences to the corporation in accelerating pension costs. Why then do we support it?

Some might point out that in the "onward and upward society," with the concept of a steady and unidirectional progression of wages for an individual, there comes a time when man out-prices himself in terms of the value he contributes to the corporate enterprise. In the jargon of the personnel world, he becomes "a red circle" case.

This is probably true to a very large degree. The "Peter principle" deals with this same phenomeon. It is even conceivable that man prices himself out of the market of his utility to the extent that his extra pension cost is less than the extra cost to carry him on payroll beyond his current real value to the corporation. This then is when we want to retire him or squeeze him out. But is this our only recourse? Or can we treat him like the product that has passed its peak demand curve? Why not downgrade man when he should be downgraded? Is not this preferable both sociologically as well as economically to dropping him out of the mainstream entirely?

Why not initiate a variable wage cycle, a wage that rises, reaches a peak, and then recedes as productive contribution itself diminishes. Additional time off could be given to an employee to compensate for reduced wages so that he may phase not only his economics toward retirement but also his life style itself.

There is a further factor to consider and that is the usefulness of having a cadre of trained familiar part-time employees on tap. Such a cadre could perhaps be expanded or contracted in terms of hours worked for the corporation more easily than the fully committed work force itself. What do we do when we need extra manpower?

Go to overtime.
Hire a temporary.
Add to staff.

Overtime involves premium pay at extra cost to the corporation. Hiring a temporary involves extra cost to the corporation in that someone else's overhead and profit factor have to be paid for as well as the basic wage itself. Adding to staff, while ostensibly the cheapest alternative, may in a short-run situation be the most expensive alternative, as we have already discussed in an earlier chapter.

But, what about a fourth alternative, namely, temporarily expanding the working hours of our cadre of part-time semiretirees? No premium is involved, no recruitment, severance, or training; involved instead is perhaps gratitude to be allowed to be more productive and to earn more pay, even if only temporarily. Is not this a possible alternative worth considering? Surely it must be. Before leaving this subject, let us review these thoughts again in the context of a specific case history of John Doe, employee of XYZ Company.

In the competitive environment of our modern industrial society, corporate success is measured in terms of growth—growth of revenues, growth of profits, growth of earnings per share. Those corporations with the best track record of dynamic and consistent growth are referred to as our "blue chips" and command a priority position in the eyes of our financial community. Psychologically, all corporate enterprises aspire toward this criterion of growth image. Some succeed; others fall by the wayside in time and are gobbled up by larger, more successful competitors, or are relegated to oblivion in some other fashion. But, in this race for corporate growth, is it likely that its people will be able to maintain a growth pattern paralleling that of the corporation itself? In terms of compensation, the answer may well be yes, at least substantially so. Bigger corporations obviously can afford to pay higher salaries for a given job, and they do so. A recent survey published by Dartnell reports that, for some 1900 companies surveyed, a corporate controller's average base pay will vary as follows:

CONTROLLER

COMPENSATION ($000)

Annual Sales Volume	Base ($) Average	Base ($) Range Middle Half	Total Compensation ($) Average	Total Compensation ($) Range Middle Half
$5 Billion Plus	60	48–78	118	94–153
$2–5 Billion	57	46–74	84	67–109
$1–2 Billion	52	42–62	69	55–83
$500 Million–1 Billion	46	37–55	57	46–68
$250–500 Million	39	31–47	47	38–56
$100–250 Million	34	27–41	43	34–52
$50–100 Million	27	19–35	33	23–43
$25–50 Million	21	15–27	27	19–35
$5–25 Million	19	15–25	24	19–31
Under $5 Million	16	13–21	18	14–23

Many similar surveys will report the same phenomenon, and for all positions of the industrial management hierarchy the same observation applies. But what of our trusted employee, John Doe, who joined the company 17 years ago? The corporation he elected to join in 1957 had sales of $15,000,000. Now, 17 years later, its sales are more than ten times that figure, and its operations are multiplant, multinational, and highly complex. This corporation has certainly grown and performed well in the industrial performance criteria mill. But what has happened to John Doe?

John Doe joined Corporation XYZ in 1957 at age 25. He had a bachelors degree in economics and a few years of experience with another company before joining XYZ Company. He was employed as a junior supervisor at $200 per week. Now, 17 years later, after a progression of middle management administrative and supervisory jobs, he holds the title of Internal Sales Supervisor at a salary of $21,000 per annum. Has John Doe grown? His salary has doubled. Some might feel this is satisfactory; others might not. John Doe is not complaining. He "found a home" at XYZ Company. But has he *grown* in these 17 years? The answer is "no, he has not"; his skills have not kept pace with the needs of the company. His technology is back a decade or more in the past. The plain fact is that he is not worth his present salary to XYZ Company. XYZ's needs are far more complex and demanding now than they were 17 years ago as a $15,000,000 company. While John Doe was what they needed at that phase of the corporate life cycle, they have outgrown John Doe and left him behind—the only thing that remains is John Doe himself and his paycheck. And what is to become of John Doe? He has been loyal; he has been conscientious and responsive to whatever the corporation called on him to do. He contributed what he was able. Salary increases have continued, but at a slower pace. John Doe does not mind that much, as long as he can reasonably keep pace with inflation. But to XYZ Company, he is not worth the $21,000 that they are paying him. They do not know how to resolve this problem. Here are the alternatives in his case:

1. Early retirement seems to be a possible way, but John Doe is only 42 years old, too young to think of retirement. Besides, retire on what? Even if he were fully vested in his pension benefits at XYZ Company, which would rarely be the case in less than 20 years, below age 55, his pension benefit at age 65 would be so materially discounted to present value at age 42 that it would not even begin to support him.

2. Does XYZ "bite the bullet" and terminate John Doe, a 17-year employee, give him a year's severance or so, and tell him to go out and start over again somewhere else that needs the skills that he can contribute. Some companies do in fact take this approach and, while it is tough initially on John Doe, and certainly it deals a blow to the morale and sense of job security of other longer-term employees of the company, the company rationalizes that over the longer term this purging process is healthier for John Doe's personal sense of pride and well being than to remain in house feeling "red circle," a noncontributing member.

This corporate attitude seems self-serving and harsh, but in a corporation that has grown tenfold, the likelihood of moving faster and beyond the abilities of some of its middle managers, and even some of its senior management, to keep up, is great. With one John Doe, there is not much pressure for a solution, but suppose you have 10 John Doe's in XYZ Company, suppose you have 100? Is this a cost that you want to carry year after year indefinitely into the future?

3. Another possible approach is to have the industrial relations people sit down and talk it over with John Doe, explain to him that further salary growth and opportunity for advancement is unlikely, and that he may wish to look outside for such goals if they are important to him. This approach would obviously be appropriate if it were done early in the game. Unfortunately, many industrial executives are guilty of constant procrastination in all forms, and failing to face up to John Doe is one of them. So nobody talks to John and he continues to get small annual increases. Slowing down salary growth, however, does not solve the problem, because XYZ Corporation is continuing to grow in size and complexity each day, and next time around John Doe is even more obsolete than he was last year. Just freezing him in place is not the answer then. XYZ Corporation would like to free up that place for a younger up-and-coming supervisor who has more enthusiasm, more energy, more new ideas, and is more qualified to get the job done and to whom this would be a step up the ladder. But John Doe is occupying the spot, and there is no other higher or lateral spot for him that he can properly fill, and the corporation is now reluctant to face up to his obsolescence because of his many years of service with the company. The agonized claim is that "John has been here too long; he knows so much about us—knowledge that others just do not have—surely in a roster of over 1000 employees there must be some place for him where this knowledge can be effectively put to use?"

'And there is such a place, very likely, but it is *down* the ladder, not sideways or up. But, why *not* put John Doe in this spot, where he can contribute something the company needs? The answer is always, "The job is not worth what we are paying John," and so the useful solution is not selected. And why is it not? Because if John Doe is put in that job and is paid $21,000 per year, the other employees in similar jobs, or even more important jobs, will all get excited because their salaries are not equal to John's. I am sure personnel directors live with this dialogue on a daily basis.

But the problem has not gone away. John Doe is still working for XYZ Company at $21,000. There does not appear to be any really good solution, so what to do?

Two thoughts occur to me:

1. Transfer John to the lower level job at the salary applicable to that job. The balance of his salary could be handled in one of three ways, depending on company policy:

   (a) Frozen and charged to a certain industrial relations cost center so that the companywide costs of "red circle" amounts can have visibility. Cost of living or perhaps even merit increases will be charged to his productive job cost center and will serve to decrease his "red circle" override charged to the industrial relations budget.

   (b) Just put it up to John that he must take the lower paying job and have his salary reduced to this level either promptly or scaled down in an orderly progression over some negotiated time. John, of course, can refuse this course and elect to go elsewhere outside.

   (c) For older employees than John Doe, employees closer to retirement age, reduced pay and more time off could be proposed on some agreed-upon program so that such employees are gradually phased down to retirement pay levels. As indicated earlier, there may well be opportunities on a short-term basis for drawing on variable services from such a cadre of part-time employees. How often do short-term programs come up that require the Industrial Relations Department to go out and hire "temps" or even go out and hire full-time people and hope that the short-term need will translate itself into a long-term need in due course of time. And what of the need to cover summer vacation workload problems? Is it not possible that the cadre of John Does or other part-timers or senior retirees could pitch in here to the company's advantage?

There are surely other techniques than these to come to grips with the problem of John Doe. At a minimum, we should know the cost of "red circle" excesses present in the corporation at any moment of time. At a minimum, we should try to identify the corporation's goals and objectives with regard to treatment of such employees. At a minimum, we should not turn away from the problem of John Doe's cost being too high and thus must be reduced in one form or another. My final thought is that in the Drone Society we seem to be striving to create in our modern day economic environment, let us not close our eyes to the opportunities of turning even man in his waning productive years, made possible by increased longevity, from a liability to yet a further residual asset.

CHAPTER 10

ARE PENSION PLANS OBSOLETE? TRENDS IN SOCIAL SECURITY BENEFITS

While significant social consciousness of the industrial enterprise is largely a development of the past 50 years, it is generally taken for granted these days that a corporation must provide a retirement benefit for its working force. Since the passage of the Social Security Act, there has been a struggle between the public sector, that is, the government, and the private sector, that is, the industrial corporation, as to the relative merits of who is responsible for administering and funding this benefit. To the extent that the benefit is provided by the government, it is "fully portable," whereas, as has been well publicized and often bitterly contested, benefits advertised as provided by the corporation itself are all too often forfeited and returned indirectly to the coffers of the corporation when an employee terminates from the company prior to normal retirement age. In such instances, the employee himself often never receives credit or other benefit for those years of service with the corporation insofar as providing for his retirement upkeep, except as provided for under the Social Security Act itself.

This is an inequity that is gradually disappearing from the corporate scene, and with the passage of current legislation before Congress, which appears likely, the death knell of unreasonable forfeiture provisions of private pension plans will have been rung. It is hard to believe that the resistance of the private sector to increased portability is a philosophical or sociological one. It has to be almost entirely economic, because, as we have shown in earlier chapters, the cost implications of shortening or eliminating vesting requirements are enormous. Hence there are real cost threats involved in this controversy which understandably has evoked a highly anguished defensive reaction on the part of industry for the many past years over which this dialogue has raged.

The reasoning of the corporate sector has been, from the start, since the birth of Social Security itself, that the corporation could not control what the politically motivated public sector would do in the field of retirement legislation, so the best the private sector could do at any point of time was to provide the vehicle for a suitable retirement benefit, adjusted upward from year to year to keep pace with competitive pressures for higher benefits as the need for such benefits was recognized in the general employment and labor market place. The corporation is on the firing line with labor, and by providing the vehicle for true retirement benefit, had to keep pace with reality. By way of protection, corporations chose the mechanism of integration with Social Security, so that as political pressures resulted in increased benefits in the public sector, these benefits would not be redundant but would be incorporated within the private sector vehicle itself. Integration with Social Security in simplest terms means that the corporation contracts for a retirement benefit of $X\$$, or $X\%$ of final pay (as defined), which benefit is *inclusive* of what the government would pay a given employee from the Social Security program. In this way, the reasoning went, if the government liberalized Social Security and legislated higher payroll levies on the corporation, as well as the employee himself (which it has in fact done), the aggregate costs of the corporation would not be pyramided, but would merely be switched from private sector costs to public sector costs paid for by the corporation itself. This was certainly a sound thesis and, as the past 40 years' record has shown, was unquestionably a wise precaution from the corporate point of view. The record of Social Security legislation has indeed shown a rather active "onward and upward" trend. There are three principal parameters whereby the public sector, through Social Security, has enlarged its economic impact:

1. Bringing more people under the jurisdiction of Social Security itself.
2. Advancing the rate of payroll levy of the Social Security tax itself.
3. Increasing the compensation base on which the current percentage rate is levied.

Item 1 is not really pertinent to the corporate concerns of this book, but items 2 and 3 definitely are. Let us see what the historic trend of change has been in each of these areas in Chart 32.

No one can doubt that this trend has been active and certainly points to further action and further economic cost burdens on both the individual and the corporate entity itself in the years ahead. But under our concept of integration, whereby the private sector incorporates to the extent allowed the increased contribution toward pension benefit of the public sector, this alone should not spell trouble for the private sector. Is this really true?

Before we consider this point, let us first look at what these public sector trends mean in themselves—what additional costs have they created, regardless

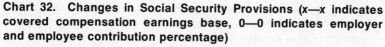

Chart 32. Changes in Social Security Provisions (x—x indicates covered compensation earnings base, 0—0 indicates employer and employee contribution percentage)

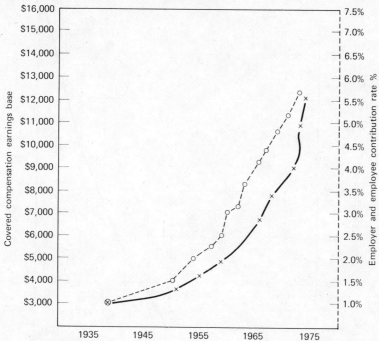

of the protective device of integration, and what additional benefits of themselves do they yield, again irrespective of the effect of integration with the private sector.

Chart 33 shows the cost trends over the years to the employee and the corporation alike, because they each share these same costs and all the cost increases alike.

And now let us see what benefits the employee will get from these increased annual contributions in Chart 34. Just what is he getting for his dollar?

Chart 35 is worth examining at this point: it shows the change in mix of how much of an employee's retirement benefit is coming from the public sector as opposed to the private sector.

This series of charts shows some very interesting trends and certainly raises some highly pertinent questions. One such question is, "Is the retirement that we are buying from our Social Security dollars commensurate with the costs of

Chart 33. History and Projection of Maximum Social Security Contributions (future based on Social Security administration assumptions)

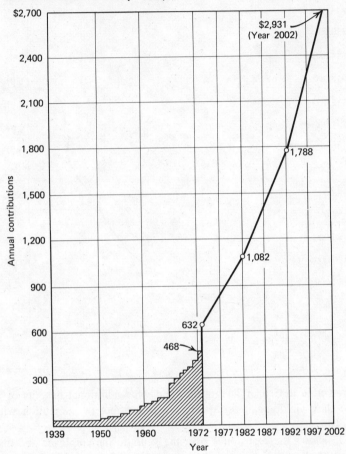

Social Security itself?'' This is a loaded question because, in posing this question, I already instinctively suspect that the answer has to be ''No,'' but let us examine the facts. In today's Social Security world, both the corporation and the employee must pay 5.85% on the first $12,600 of annual compensation. This means together we are buying from Uncle Sam for a $12,600 a year employee, an 11.7% of compensation pension benefit. In the private sector, this would buy this employee, aged 25, a retirement benefit at age 65 of $1,284 per

Chart 34. History and Projection of Maximum Primary Social Security Benefit (future based on Social Security administration assumptions)

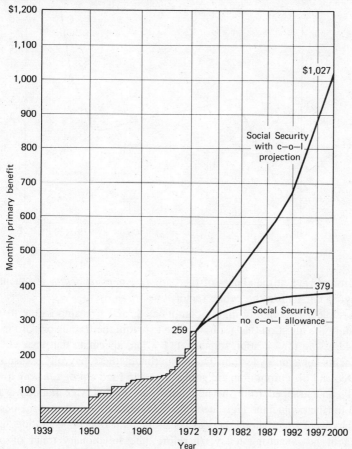

month. Why, then, will he only get $657 per month from Social Security as Chart 36 indicates?

I wonder how many persons are aware of this question, either as individuals or as corporate financial men? Probably not very many; yet the question is valid. It implies a basic theoretical inefficiency in the public sector that affects both the employee and the corporation alike. Both could claim with some justice that they are not getting their money's worth and that the very politicians

Chart 35.   How Much of an Employee's Retirement Benefit Comes from Public Versus Private Sector?

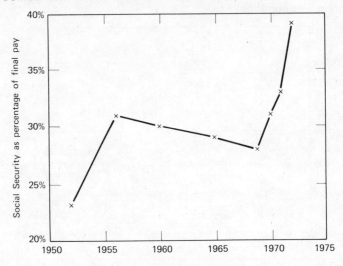

who rant and rave at the abuses of the corporate pension sector are themselves not playing fair ball in the public sector.

This subject is certainly highly complicated, and it is impossible to answer adequately the question that we have posed, within the framework of this book. But, addressing the question somewhat, I would speculate that instead of buying benefits for employee John Doe as outlined, these payroll assessments on John Doe and his corporation are going in part to fund a program which was essentially bootstrapped from the beginning—no past service liability was ever funded for the people and legislated into Social Security, either at the beginning or as they were added along the way. Nor did John Doe, a generation ago, buy the benefit he is getting today; therefore, the inflationary trend of pension benefits were not funded in a historic perspective. This being true, they must be funded in today's world by John Doe, Jr.

This means that John Doe, Jr. will not get the pension benefit he is paying for, unless, by the good graces of future politicians, John Doe III and his future corporation pick up the tab. While this appears to be the political game plan, as a present-day financial strategist, I am not sure that either John Doe, Jr., or I feel very comfortable about this.

Let us ask ourselves another important question now. If as Chart 35 shows, the trend has been for the public sector to provide an increasingly greater share of an employee's retirement benefit, is there any reason to believe that this

Chart 36.   What Does Social Security Buy in Monthly Retirement Benefits? [Assumed: On January 1, 1974 a worker, age 25, joins work force. His salary is $12,600 and no salary increases are projected. He retires at 65; his wife is also 65 at his retirement. *Note:* This table only includes monthly retirement payments. Social Security benefits are more comprehensive than this—the trust fund benefits are not.)

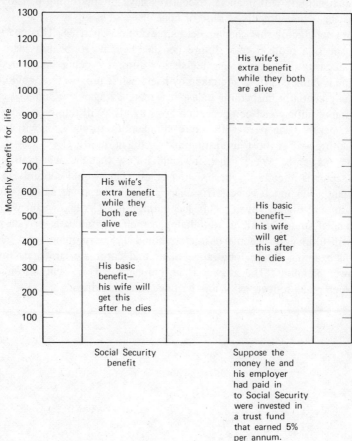

trend will be reversed, or even confined? I can hardly doubt it. If so, the trend will continue, and as it does, it becomes clear that the public sector will exert continuing pressure on the private pension sector until the future day when the public sector assumes the entire responsibility, and the private sector is no longer involved except insofar as custodianship and distribution of past contributions into the now defunct corporate pension trust. When this happens, how much latitude will financial executives have in controlling pension costs? The answer is undoubtedly, "little or none"!

Before concluding this chapter, let us reexamine Chart 34. This chart shows the prospective projection of future pension benefits to be provided by the Social Security program under legislation currently being considered. This trend line is rather startling and taken by itself, while provocative, could be criticized as potentially misleading unless it is matched against a similar trend line projection of anticipated compensation level trends. Will future Social Security benefits merely keep pace with future compensation trends, or will they outstrip such trends? A most interesting and pertinent question!

If the answer is "Yes," then it would follow that the acceleration of the public sector is already on the drawing board. This would certainly make the accountant's job much easier. His charge against corporate earnings for pension costs will merely revert to his accounting for FICA taxes. But what about the financial strategist? If, as this dialogue seems to indicate, private pension plans will ultimately become obsolete, should this development not be anticipated in examing future long-range plans and corporate strategies involving manpower planning? The answer is an emphatic "Yes," but I wonder how many such plans reflect, as of this writing, such thinking.

CHAPTER II

THE ROLE OF INCENTIVES AND PROFIT SHARING

No book on the financial cost considerations of man can be complete without some discussion of the role of incentives. As indicated in an earlier chapter, extra compensation provided by incentives, in many instances, becomes the catalyst whereby man's obsolescence becomes feasible.

Actually, incentives are so varied and so dynamic that they could be the subject of a book by themselves. This chapter cannot possibly cover the consequences of all the wide variety of present-day incentive alternatives, but, at best, can only refer to them superficially. Nevertheless, I feel that the book would be incomplete without some discussion, and, as most authors do, I suppose, I have a personal axe to grind—a pet theory on a future trend possibility of retirement funding—that needs a discussion on incentives to set the stage.

Why have incentives? What function do they serve for the corporate enterprise? Certainly, the "carrot" has been around for quite a few years now, and incentives are not a new phenomenon.

There are two basic rationales to having incentives, in my opinion. One, and the most obvious and predominant one, is the desire to stimulate productivity or achievement, which will basically yield a greater economic benefit to the corporation; hence some of this incremental benefit can be offered as a reward to the person or persons whose performance is required to bring this about. The classic example is, of course, found in blue collar production bonus plans. For a given job, a worker is given a basic wage for achieving a basic defined "task." If, within a given time frame, he exceeds this task, he earns a bonus above basic wage. The more production above task, the higher this bonus and the greater his take-home pay—the old carrot! As his take-home pay increases, the per unit production cost of the article he is producing declines, providing decreased costs and better margins for his corporation. Certainly a good deal is gained by both parties, if the task and bonus increments are set fairly and intelligently. This is probably the most common incentive for the rank and file employee himself.

For the executive, or senior executive, there may be other forms of incentive less specific in terms of quid pro quo. The "good guys–bad guys" discretionary bonus is probably the most common incentive in this category. While this may well be the bane of the Personnel Director's existence in terms of discriminatory practices and their impact upon the morale of the organization, it still, nevertheless, is a potent motivating force.

The old adage still applies:

> Love makes the world go around.
> I do not care;
> It's cash I've always found
> That makes things square.

So here we have the extremes—on the one hand, a highly structured cash incentive measured in specific terms by daily performance—on the other hand, a highly unstructured cash incentive measured in unspecific terms by subjective discretion of each participant's performance. Both are incentives, and useful and powerful ones, each in its own way. In between, are a myriad of other incentives of differing specifications, but, generally, of the same nature. Some of the more popular of these are as follows:

Commissions
Deferred compensation agreements
Stock options (qualified or unqualified)
Tandem options
Phantom options
Performance shares
Profit sharing—Cash
Deferred profit sharing

Of these, perhaps two, that is, commissions and performance shares, may be structured to relate in some degree to variable individual performance measurement, whereas the rest are assigned to an individual either in consideration of past performance or projected future performance of the individual. The size of the incentive may be geared to this assessment, but the measure of the incentive value itself is not related to individual response, but to the group response, of the entire company usually. This is true with forms of options (other than, perhaps, performance shares), and it is true with various forms of profit sharing formulas, also.

From an accounting viewpoint, all of these plans are pretty much similar; that is, the charge against current earnings is the cost to the company at the point of time when a fixed and formal liability to the benefit is determined.

With profit sharing, it is the amount per the Board of Directors resolution, if discretionary, or the audited formula, presuming payment into the trust prior to payment of Federal Income Tax, if a formula plan.

For options, "when the liability is fixed," is related to vesting provision and to actual exercise of the option itself except for phantom stock and performance shares. Unvested options or unexercised options are required to be footnoted, but constitute no charge against earnings per share until or unless exercised. The charge against earnings here would be the specified value of the option price, irrespective of market value, unless present laws change in this regard, and stock options have been and continue to be under considerable pressure from the SEC.

Phantom stock is like a cash bonus that is measured by a stock price formula, rather than some other formula. I do not believe that it is very popular at the present time, because it offers no real advantages over a cash bonus and, being tied to a temporary market value of the company's stock price, may have some real and unrelated temporary disadvantages at a given point of time that defeat the objective of the incentive.

Performance shares, similar to phantom options, offer no tax advantage and are only unique in that they may bridge the gap between individual performance of a unit of the company and total company performance. In many cases, performance shares may be offered to a given individual executive to achieve a certain performance goal in a given year. A comparable cash bonus could do the same thing. Company shares, however, are selected to remind the executive that, in addition to the fulfillment of his individual goals, he, nevertheless, continues to be a member of the management team and must be a party also to the success or failure of the total company goals, as well as his own. Hence shares of company stock, instead of cash, are his reward. From an accounting standpoint, as with phantom stock, the cost of his shares to the company, being a fully taxable transaction, is the market value on the date his entitlement to the shares becomes fixed. The company can still, I believe, fix its cost of such shares by buying and using treasury shares at cost, in any given year, but to be useful this assumes a rising market price of the shares. Many articles on performance shares point out the disadvantage of increased dilution, but, while this is true, it must be weighed as a practical matter against the relative number of shares totally issued and outstanding by the company. No matter what form of option plan is used, if such is the chosen form of incentive, it comes down to the cost over a period of years to achieve an improved result— and does this cost, conversely, achieve a proper motivational response with the executives involved?

Deferred compensation contracts is another popular form of incentive. This is a form of cash bonus with strings attached. The strings, of course, are necessary to achieve the deferred tax objectives which is the essential purpose of such plans. It is probably true that most executive incentive plans try to reward the executive in some tax-free, tax-deferred, or tax-reduced manner that provides him an attractive benefit, net of tax. Let us face it; cash would do the same thing, as many corporations are now finding to an increasing degree. The executive does not care about the tax gimmicks; he just cares about what it will yield to him *net*.

Unfortunately, the corporation that pays him does care, and is concerned about saving its earnings per share and having Uncle Sam pick up part of the tab for motivating the executive. Hence, there is a lot of wheeling and dealing, tax lawyers' delights, and such, to accomplish all this. Although the objective is a good one, it is frequently abused. And why would not Uncle Sam, as well as Corporation X, be equally interested in motivating executive John Doe to help create more profits? More profits for Corporation X should be good for Corporation X, and taxes on those profits should, likewise, be good for Uncle Sam; so why all these tax games and gimmicks? The logic is somewhat elusive except for abuse control, in which event I would have to agree with the logic.

Before leaving the subject of the use of company stock as an incentive, I would like to expand more fully on the subject of performance shares, because this is a fairly new concept and is not widely known as yet, and because I have been personally intrigued with it and have selected it as the executive incentive device to be developed in my present business association. I have used the word "developed" advisedly, because the word "performance" implies not only the concept of "measurement" but also, and perhaps more importantly, the concept of "objective." A performance shares program carries with it a desire on the part of the corporation to define for each of its top executives in specific terms what the corporation expects each one to achieve. Also the corporation must define for itself, as well as for each executive, the degree of achievement in each of these measurements that constitutes acceptable performance, with ranges from mediocre to outstanding. The shares awards are then tailored to these individual corporate goals and are apportioned within each goal along the degrees of acceptable performance. All this sounds easy, but I would bet that for most corporations it is far from easy and that to vocalize and measure effectively such goals in such specific terms may well take vigorous soul-searching dialogues and may even take a period of years to refine and sophisticate adequately. This is certainly true in my present experience. In spite of this fact, I personally feel that it is worth the effort and that corporations should not back off from the serious study and definition of exactly what they require of each of their top executives. Nor is this a one-way unilateral dialogue. To be effective, the top executive to be measured must agree substantially that such performance goals and degrees of achievement criteria are in fact realistic and equitable. In a sense, then, a performance shares plan is an understanding that the corporation enters into annually with each of its senior executives as to what specifically he will undertake to produce for the corporation during the year that meets the corporation goals for growth. Is it not far better from the stockholder's viewpoint to know that senior management will only be rewarded if something well-defined and tangible has been achieved for the direct benefit of the stockholders? You can be sure that there are many stock option plans and other executive incentive plans that do not yield this satisfaction to the stockholder.

Viewing the subject more specifically, let us examine for each of the corporation's top executives what kinds of goals might be considered. Obviously, each corporation will be somewhat unique and will have to define these concepts for itself rather than accept any generalized yardsticks developed by others.

CHIEF EXECUTIVE, CHIEF OPERATING, AND CHIEF FINANCIAL OFFICERS

Obviously, this is the easiest objective to vocalize and measure. The corporation and its stockholders look to these officers to increase earnings per share. But what rate of growth is acceptable—5, 10, or 15%? If 15% is considered to be the norm, at what point does incentive begin, and below which point is no incentive at all for these officers? And if 15% is the norm selected, does the executive get full reward for 15% growth, or 90 or 80% of his reward for just meeting the norm? All of these questions must be seriously examined and agreed on before a performance shares plan can commence, or, if commenced, can then be considered as mature and debugged. But do you not feel that this dialogue is worthwhile and more than just an exercise? I, for one, certainly do.

There are other dimensions to this simplest of measurements. For worldwide multinationals, for companies using tax-haven strategies, is an aftertax profits measurement the only proper one to use? You may decide, perhaps, that half of your executive's benefit should be geared to worldwide pretax performance growth and the other half geared to preserving the tax strategies or aftertax profits growth.

DIVISIONAL HEADS AND SENIOR MARKETING HEADS

These executives are given P&L responsibility for certain segments of the business. Obviously, they are fairly easily measured in terms of the performance of each of their divisions. But here, again, a number of questions must be posed and answered before a performance shares plan can be fairly and properly implemented.

1. Must all divisions be tied to the same profit growth goals as the total corporation? If so, this will discourage or penalize divisions that by their nature may not have the same profit rate opportunity as other divisions. Is this fair, and is it to the stockholders best interest to discourage entry into peripheral divisions whose profit growth may be incrementally attractive to the corporation, but whose growth rates on a "stand alone basis" would not fit the profile of the company's dominant activities?
2. Do you use the same growth criteria for new divisions as you do for more mature divisions?
3. What P&L do you wish to measure? Controllable divisional contribution before corporate overhead allocations, or "fully loaded" bottom-line pretax?
4. Do you only wish to measure for a given year the P&L contribution, or do you wish to divide the incentive and allocate a portion to the development of new business that will affect future years?
5. While a divisional entity in many cases may be fairly autonomous, what effect do you wish to allow, if any, for noncontrollable factors impacting on divisional performance, that is, failure or delay of new product introductions, manufacturing plant or procurement problems, and strikes?

These are some of the more pertinent questions to be resolved in implementing a performance shares plan. There are obviously others.

CHIEF MANUFACTURING OFFICER

The corporation obviously expects such an executive to deliver product to its divisional heads in such quantities and times as have been demanded and agreed on in the formulation of the future business plans for the corporation that form the basis for determining and measuring the performance shares of all of its executives. But quantity and timing of delivery are only two of this executive's mandates. Cost and quality are of equal importance. Therefore, the corporation really expects this executive to deliver to its Marketing Divisions a certain dollar volume of gross manufacturing profit margin. This would presume that performance shares can easily be geared to growth of manufacturing gross profit dollars paralleling the corporation's growth goals. Not true! Life is not that simple, I am afraid. Let us suppose the following:

1. One or more marketing divisions fail to produce the forecast for incoming orders. This, in turn, impacts on the manufacturing executive's production schedules, perhaps also on his inventory turnover performance. Should he be penalized for failing to deliver these profit margin dollars?
2. New product introductions are delayed by pilot run problems, debugging, delays and higher costs due to ECN's, higher rework costs to correct parts and update to latest revision, and such. Is the manufacturing executive to be held accountable for these problems?

SENIOR EXECUTIVE RESPONSIBLE FOR ACQUISITIONS

The executive charged with responsibility for external growth should be easy to measure—either he consummates deals or he does not. On the surface, this sounds easy, but here, again, there are a number of parameters that must first be defined:

1. What growth rate of external acquisitions has been defined within the corporation's long-range game plan.
2. Presumably, criteria for acceptable acquisitions has been well vocalized and the senior executive charged with this responsibility merely must identify candidates that fit such criteria and (hopefully) negotiate deals.
3. Is the executive measured on revenue growth provided by acquisitions, or on pretax profit growth of companies acquired, or is his incentive performance divided between the two?
4. Some acquisisitions take many months, perhaps even years, to consummate. What serves as the basis for performance for an executive who works hard all year to consummate an acquisition and brings it in in December, signed sealed and delivered; has he performed?
5. Is he responsible for performance of the new acquisition after the "marriage ceremony" when perhaps you have a "weeping bride," the disenchanted bridesmaids have fled to parts unknown, and the groom's hungry divisional marketing executives have moved in like vultures to cannibalize what they can for their own divisional growth needs?

SENIOR EXECUTIVE RESPONSIBLE FOR PRODUCT ENGINEERING AND DEVELOPMENT

This measurement is a "real one" and many will claim that it defies measurement. You simply can not measure research! When product development constitutes a major effort in your company and commands a major portion of your budgeted expenditures, such an answer simply is not good enough. The effectiveness of research *must* be measured somehow. Just "living within" the budget is not good enough. The corporation and its stockholders need to know what they are getting for these dollars and that these dollars are worth spending.

In the final analysis, the corporation looks to its chief product development executive to develop and deliver new product and if he does so in some time frame, he has fulfilled this goal; if not, he has failed. Admittedly, the time frame cannot be a short-term one because most product development is measured in terms of years rather than in terms of months. But does this fact frustrate measurement? I do not believe so.

The corporation first must define what its internal growth needs and goals are in similar manner to its external definitions. Such internal needs may be in a variety of forms, but they come down to the following:

1. What dollar growth rate of new products shipped forms the basis for the internal development mandate?
2. What relative percentage of a corporation's annual revenues are targeted to be the result of new product introductions (i.e., defined, perhaps, as products placed in pilot production within the past two fiscal years).

   Therefore, if a corporation should wish its product line to turn over every five years, it would establish a goal for new product introductions to average 20% on a moving average basis. As corporate growth rose in accordance with its growth goals (perhaps 15% per year), in similar fashion the dollars yielded by the product development goals would be constantly rising in proportionate manner. It is in his ability to meet this challenge that the chief product development executive must be measured.

There are other executives that could be discussed here, and I could go into greater detail in discussing each one, but I feel that the objective of this dialogue has already been achieved—to give the reader some of the flavor of the involvement necessary to implement an executive performance shares plan.

I, for one, feel that such involvement is entirely justified and is, in fact, critical to the mature forward growth of today's industrial enterprise. Companies that do not ask themselves these same questions and do not try to develop satisfactory answers, whether in response to a performance shares incentive or not, are simply avoiding the basics that may well spell success or failure in the corporation's future development.

Let us take a look at profit sharing plans. Such plans are not new to the American industrial scene and many have been in existence for 20 years or more. The concept of profit sharing may be egalitarian to a degree, but it is more likely that it is motivated by corporate self-interest; hence it is basically a form of group incentive plan. The better the company prospers, the more of a pie is available to divide among the employees. Some plans are discretionary and the mechanism by which the variable profit sharing payout is determined, while based on the current year's profit performance, still rests on the subjective decision of the Board of Directors as to what tangible form this recognition of profit performance will take. I think the more promising plans, however, relate to a formula that can be known in advance, respected as a fair task by the employees, and followed with interest throughout the year by those employees. In such a plan, if employees generally know that after a certain amount of profit has been earned, usually called a capital deduction for invested capital, they will start receiving a certain predetermined percentage of the profits of the company, perhaps 10%, maybe 25%, and in some rare instances even as high as 40 or 50%, this knowledge can act as a powerful motivating force, which, of course, is the purpose of the plan. If top managements can get across the idea effectively to the working and managerial population of their companies that after the basic wages of the stockholder, that is the deduction for capital, has been earned, a certain portion of every additional dollar earned in a profit improvement program, or conversely, a certain portion of every additional expense dollar saved in productivity or cost reduction program, goes directly into the employee's or supervisor's own pocket, this can be a powerful motivational tool. The effectiveness of management's ability to communicate the profit sharing religious fervor is critical. I am sure there is an abundant history of companies that have failed in the communication task, and hence have realized little or no motivational impact out of their profit sharing concepts. On the other hand, where companies have bridged the communications barrier with employees effectively, they have created often a militancy among their employees that can be startling, if not even overwhelming.

The records speak eloquently of companies like Sears Roebuck and Montgomery Ward, to name a few, where profit sharing has reaped major termination benefits for long service employees, and where, obviously, the profit sharing concept has been probably not *an* important fringe benefit, but *the most* important fringe benefit that such companies have to offer to induce employees to join their particular company, to motivate them to work effectively for its prosperity, and to discourage them from departing for greener pastures elsewhere.

But there are also other companies where the profit sharing experience has been a disaster and has left a bad taste in the mouths of employees who feel that management sold them a bill of goods on empty illusions that did not, in fact, reward them for their faith and their efforts, but produced instead the devastation of such inputs by stupid and costly management errors beyond the understanding or control of the rank and file profit sharing members themselves.

Thus you see, there can be two sides to this picture.

Some professional advisers will caution against profit sharing as an incentive mechanism, and will claim that there is no statistical evidence to prove that companies with profit sharing plans are any more successful than similar companies without profit sharing plans. If this is so, then, they claim that companies that do offer broad-based profit sharing are really wasting their money and could achieve better effectiveness by selecting more focussed major incentives directed to a smaller group of key personnel.

I am sure that this claim would be hotly disputed by many, but the merits of the profit sharing incentive will not be settled by this chapter, nor is it my intention to try to do so.

By way of illustration, I think it would be useful to show the objective of a typical formula profit sharing plan under differing conditions. You must realize that there are a wide variety of formulas and features of profit sharing plans, but the purpose here is to illustrate to the financial reader the purpose of the profit sharing incentive as a motivating force in aiding profit growth achievement for the corporation. Let us see how XYZ Corporation can be affected in Chart 37.

The bare figures in Chart 37 are hypothetical and you could substitute virtually any base you wish for purposes of this model. However, taking the figures as they are, it can be seen that variable bonuses of this company under this formula can be reduced or wiped out if performance deteriorates and, conversely, there can be reward for improved performance where profits go up. In this latter example, a $400,000 additional profit sharing payment, equated to a bonus increase of 4.5% on compensation, will produce an earnings per share increase of 32 ¢, a market value per share increase of $3.20, and an aggregate market value increase of the company of $8,000,000.

In this context, the company has given a reward to employees of 5¢ for each additional paper profit dollar earned by the stockholders. Construed in this light, profit sharing, if properly structured, can be a dynamic tool for the benefit both of employee and shareholder alike. One further fact worth noting here is that, under this formula, the employees must provide earnings growth for the shareholders merely to continue to earn the same variable bonus. In the final column, it can be seen that the retained earnings of the corporation have increased from prior year. This means that, before profit sharing begins, the employee must earn first a basic wage for the additional investment the stockholder has allowed to remain at the disposal of the corporation. In this example, to earn the same 7.4% bonus, the employee must increase earnings per share from 86 to 91¢. Market price of the stock on this basis should rise from $8.60 to $9.10 and aggregate market value of the company should increase by $1,250,000, all this before profit sharing is increased at all. This should point

Chart 37. Illustration of Profit Sharing Formula (Based on Revenues of $30,000,000)

	Base Figures	What if Profits Go Down	What if Profits Go Down Still Further	What if Profits Go Up	What About Same Profit Level Next Year	What to do to Earn the Same Bonus
Audited pretax profit of:	$5,000,000	$3,000,000	$0	$7,000,000	$5,000,000	$5,223,000
Allocate first a basic return to stockholders on invested capital in the business—$16,600,000 × 10%	−1,660,000	−1,660,000	−1,660,000	−1,660,000	−1,883,000	−1,883,000
Net available for profit sharing	$3,340,000	$1,340,000	$0	$5,340,000	$3,117,000	$3,340,000
Share profits at 20%	$668,000	$268,000	$0	$1,068,000	$623,000	668,000
Annual compensation base of eligible employees	$9,000,000	$9,000,000	$9,000,000	$9,000,000	$9,000,000	$9,000,000
Variable profit sharing as percentage of compensation	7.4%	3.0%	0	11.9%	6.9%	7.4%
Earnings per share after profit sharing and taxes, based upon 2,500,000 shares outstanding	86¢	55¢	0¢	$1.18	88¢	91¢

up the necessity that no profit sharing plan designed for true incentive value alone should allow an unfair windfall or penalty to the employee. If this is allowed to happen, the credibility of the plan is suspect, and its incentive motivation sapped or destroyed.

Before leaving the role of profit sharing, let me describe briefly the various forms of profit sharing plans. The common key variables are as follows:

Annual contribution—discretionary versus formula.
Distribution—in cash or to a deferred trust.
Vesting—either outright or over a period of years.

This is somewhat oversimplified, but I believe that, apart from a larger discussion of profit sharing, which the subject really deserves, these key points will cover the most commonly found parameters in significant use today.

Annual Contribution

While it would be a mistake to say that purely discretionary plans are not common, it is my view that such plans do not provide the proper basis for incentive motivation. Paternalistically oriented companies like the freedom, flexibility, and perhaps even the psychological God-image, of declaring, at their discretion each year, that the annual profit sharing contribution (usually with some reference to profit performance for the year) will be $X\%$ of compensation. Other companies relate the profit sharing pie to a certain percentage of profits for the year, but, then, once the pie is determined, they divide it up subjectively on the basis of merit among the employees. Such plans, being discriminatory, do not qualify for tax advantages; hence they are cash plans. Still other companies fix the profit sharing as a certain percentage of compensation, as guided by the allowable tax code, so that they can get a certain fixed percentage of employees' compensation qualified for deferred tax advantages, irrespective of whether profits in a given year are good, bad, or indifferent. In my view, such plans are not incentive plans because they have little motivational value. Once a fixed benefit is given on a regular basis, it becomes accepted as "one's due" by the employee, for which his only obligation in return is to exist and to continue to remain an employee. At the other end of the spectrum are formula plans, some highly structured, some more simplified. It is important that these plans be simple enough to be understood by rank and file employees, and it is essential that they be fair. While it is too much for employees to ask that such formulas only relate to economics within their control, which is an impossibility, usually, even for management employees, it is, nevertheless, necessary that plans be designed to be as reasonable and fair as possible, minimizing arbitrary decisions to alter the formula. Oddly enough, in my experience, most employees painfully but willingly accept bonuses which vary in some obviously parallel fashion with the published fortunes of their company. It is only when the parallelism is obscure or grotesque that true grumbling becomes a serious risk.

Cash Versus Deferred Trust

It is hard to find employees who are not motivated by cash, and many profit sharing plans recognize this and distribute in this manner; but, over the years, particularly with supervisory and managerial employees, the desire has been to seek ways of reducing the tax bite on incentive compensation, thus making available to such employees higher realizable benefits, after taxes, than merely a straight cash payout. All manner of deferred compensation arrangements and deferred profit sharing plans have followed this line of reasoning, and I would say this has been the more popular form of incentive plan over recent years. Very recently, straight cash seems to be rearing its ugly head again, and perhaps the pendulum is swinging back to simplicity, but it has a long way yet to go. Deferred plans, whether discretionary or formula determined, result in contributions made by the company directly into a qualified profit sharing trust for the benefit of employees. There are careful rules on how this must be done not to be discriminatory in favor of higher paid employees, and the IRS must be satisfied before proper "qualification" for deferred tax treatment is awarded to the plan. The objective is that money, put in the trust by the employer, while immediately tax deductible by the employer, is, nevertheless, not taxable to the employee until he receives an ultimate payout from the trust. Furthermore, future earnings of such sums, whether in the form of dividends, interest, or capital appreciation, are not taxed until ultimately paid out to the employee, and the payout to the employee takes place only when he terminates, retires, or dies. Under certain circumstances, such ultimate distributions may have capital gains treatment, but the rules on this have recently become more complex and less favorable and they are likely to become even more so in the years ahead. In spite of this, there remain still some valid economic reasons to recommend the deferred profit sharing trust. One is that the employee has pretax dollars invested and working for him, which is important, and the second is that for employees whose compensation falls under the maximum for FICA, both he, as an individual, and the corporation as a corporation, save and escape the FICA tax on this incremental deferred compensation by placing it into the deferred trust. This particular point, while minor, is often overlooked, both by individuals and by financial executives of the corporation itself. Do not overlook it!

Vesting Versus Nonvesting

Here, again, there is a wide range of differences between plans. Cash plans, of course, are all fully vested. Probably most deferred plans have some form of vesting period, perhaps five years, perhaps even up to ten. I would think it rare to see a plan with deferred profit sharing vesting beyond 10 years. The objective here, of course, is the old "golden handcuffs" philosophy—to tie the employee to the corporation and make it distasteful for him to leave for greener pastures elsewhere. Again, as in vested pension benefits, employees who terminate before the vesting period matures forfeit their unvested benefits which are, in the case of profit sharing plans, reallocated to the accounts of the remaining employees. Carried to its most grotesque conclusion, under such plans, managements could conceivably fire all but themselves and reallocate all unvested profit sharing contributions to themselves. I have always had a personal antipathy to vesting provisions in profit sharing plans, where the motivation is intended as an incentive plan. It has always seemed absurd to me to tell employees to go out and earn a profit sharing incentive which, when they terminate a few years later, you then claim they did not really earn, or deserve, so you take it away from them. What kind of an incentive is that? Vesting in a serious profit sharing incentive plan is entirely incompatible, in my view. However, there are many who would disagree. I think the distinction should be made between a corporate motive for true incentive versus a corporate motive instead for a variable deferred benefit. It has been the function of this chapter to deal with incentives. In the next chapter, the legitimate merits of the variable deferred benefit are examined.

CHAPTER 12

PROFIT SHARING AS A VARIABLE PENSION BENEFIT

In Chapter 11 we discussed briefly, and perhaps, superficially, the role of supplemental benefit plans. The dialogue of Chapter 11 was primarily on the incentive value of such plans. There is an additional feature of incentive plans, however, which arises out of perhaps an entirely different motivation, namely, the desire for a variable benefit as opposed to a fixed commitment. This is not to say that such plans have discarded any interest in incentive value; this is just not so; it means rather that there is yet an additional motive other than to provide an employee incentive, one that supersedes whatever incentive value a particular plan might have, namely variability. It is easy to be generous when you are rich. However, if you are not sure whether you are rich or whether new found prosperity will endure, it is only natural to try to be generous, but, at the same time, try to hedge on generosity. Such is the role, oftentimes, of deferred profit sharing plans. Discretionary plans, as contrasted with structured formula plans, must surely be motivated by a desire for flexibility or variability. What management is really saying is, "Yes, we want to share profits with you employees, but we do not want to do so if it will financially embarrass the company. We cannot foresee all the pitfalls that may develop over the career of this particular company; thus we want to protect the company from fixed arbitrary mechanisms which cannot be responsive to unforeseen corporate needs without the appearance of rescission of the employee benefit and much trauma and erosion of morale. The value of a predetermined structured benefit is just not worth the risk."

While this argument holds true, certainly, for bonuses and profit sharing plans, it is not illogical to assume that it holds true for pension benefits as well. For an emerging maturing corporation of any size, the undertaking of a pension plan is an awesome thing in itself, particularly after discussions with actuaries who point out, in rather stark terms, the monolithic nature of the commitment. It is, therefore, not unreasonable for corporations who are "dipping their toe"

123

Chart 38. Illustration of Variable Profit Sharing Versus Fixed Pension (Based on Revenues of $30,000,000)

	Base Figures	What if Profits Go Down	What if Profits Go Down Still Further	What if Profits Go Up	What About Same Profit Level Next Year	What to do to Earn the Same Bonus
Audited pretax profit, before pension expense	$5,000,000	$3,000,000	$0	$7,000,000	$5,000,000	$5,217,000
Pension cost at 7% of $9,000,000 (annual compensation base of eligible employees)	−630,000	−630,000	−630,000	−630,000	−630,000	−630,000
Pretax profit	$4,370,000	$2,370,000	$−630,000	$6,370,000	$4,370,000	$4,587,000
Aftertax profits	$2,185,000	$1,185,000	$−315,000	$3,185,000	$2,185,000	$2,243,000
What the employees get						
Variable profit sharing as percentage of compensation						
Individual year	7.4%	3.0%	0	11.9%	6.9%	7.4%
Cumulative average	7.4%	5.2%	3.5%	5.6%	5.8%	6.1%
Fixed pension as percentage of compensation	7.0%	7.0%	7.0%	7.0%	7.0%	7.0%
Effect upon earnings per share						
Variable profit sharing	86¢	55¢	0¢	$1.18	88¢	91¢
Fixed pension plan	88¢	48¢	−13¢	$1.28	88¢	90¢

into the cold water of pension commitments to want to retain some measure of variability. This can be certainly achieved by discretionary deferred profit sharing plans, and can usually be achieved adequately by formula deferred profit sharing plans, which, of course, can always be amended if circumstances require.

This point should be very simple to illustrate in Chart 38 which parallels the illustration in the preceding chapter. If we take the same set of assumptions and replace the variable profit sharing plan with a fixed pension plan equivalent to 7% of compensation, the results in Chart 38 can be compared with the earlier illustration.

These results should speak for themselves and, while an illustration such as this cannot be construed to be generally applicable, it should demonstrate at least that to the financial executive of this particular corporation, a note of caution might well be understandable in embracing the commitment inherent in a new fixed pension benefit.

People do not normally equate deferred profit sharing plans with pension benefits, but let us take a look at how their features could stack up. Of course, you should recognize that all features are variables by and large, so changing the variables is not that much of a problem for initial plan design. It could be more of a problem once the design is firm and announced. Employees naturally tend to be suspicious when plan design is altered after the fact. In such cases, it

Chart 39. Comparative Features of Deferred Profit Sharing Plan Versus Pension Plan

Deferred Profit Sharing	Pension
Variable benefit; may be better than pension plan or worse; incentive	Fixed benefit; regardless of profits of any given year; security
Forfeitures benefit employee; increase employee's fund	Forfeitures benefit company; reduce future contributions to fund
Generally more liberal short term vesting does not penalize transient	Vesting less liberal; geared to long term employees; penalizes transient
No commitment to employee on retirement amount	Contractual commitment to employee; retirement amount determined by formula
Often a loan provision	No loan provision
Sometimes can be paid in lump sum	Rarely available as lump sum

is my experience that complete honesty as to company motivations should be communicated to them because, more often than not, they identify with real company problems, and the risk of credibility in company motivation is rarely worth the gamble of displaying less than the truth. Others may feel differently, so the advice above is subjective. Let us look at possible comparative features of fixed commitment pension plans and variable commitment deferred profit sharing plans in Chart 39.

What are the advantages of going the deferred profit sharing route?

1. First and foremost, the feature of complete variability is a real protection to the immature or volatile corporation that is not sure of the stability of its earnings base, nor of its long-range capability to sustain a fixed commitment year by year without risk of embarrassment to the management and its stockholders.

2. From an employee's standpoint, a deferred profit sharing trust makes available the mechanism of reallocating forfeitures, for employees who have terminated before full vesting, to the benefit of those employees who remain. This can provide a very powerful additional incentive not present in the conventional pension trust. In conventional pension trusts, as we have seen, forfeitures are not allocated for the benefit of continuing employees but serve instead to reduce the future pension contribution of the company itself into the trust.

3. From an employer's standpoint, a formula profit sharing plan, designed to provide a pension benefit offers the employer at least the opportunity of designing a productivity requirement for improved pension benefits. Without this mechanism, as in the case of fixed pension benefits, there is no incentive for increased productivity; all given benefits soon become "built in" to the assumed fringe benefit package and do not require "reearning" each year. Instead, the corporation is confronted with the attitude, "What have you done for me lately?" and is susceptible to bargaining, whether directly or indirectly, year after year, to improve the pension benefit. On the other hand, once the philosophy of "shared profits" has been established with employees, unless the basic formula itself is unsound, it is less likely that they will demand round after progressive round of benefit increases because they already know that the profits of the company, and their own productivity towards such profits, do not support such a position.

4. When an employer is contributing for retirement benefits into a trust, monies which cannot find their way back to him, he has, for practical purposes, charged historic earnings per share for the monies that have been contributed. (This may not be true with regard to past service liabili-

ties of pension plans, but for all practical purposes, it can be generally taken as valid.) There is no real urgency on the part of the corporation, then, to "recoup" such past charges against earnings, if such were possible; so for a given dollar or percentage of compensation contribution into the trust, there is a tendency to be somewhat more liberal in terms of vesting with deferred profit sharing plans than with pension plans. This point certainly argues well for the employees in choosing a deferred profit sharing trust. I believe it can be readily established that deferred profit sharing trusts, for the most part, have vesting provisions which normally range from 5 to 15 years. There are exceptions, of course, beyond this range on either side of it, but they are the abnormal fringe, I believe. With pension plans, however, as the newspapers abundantly testify these days, there are not a few cases where vesting is not even present until death or retirement. This is a shocking phenomenon and one which I have no doubt will be corrected by Congress within the next year, but even after Congress has corrected the abuses of inadequate vesting, the pension legislation at best will require vesting which is still, I believe, far less liberal than the present range of most deferred profit sharing plans. Hence for the employees, another vote for deferred profit sharing rather than pension trust.

5. Another advantage to employees, and to the employer as well, is that deferred profit sharing plans frequently incorporate a loan provision whereby employees with an emergency need that cannot be accommodated by recourse to normal banking channels can apply for relief by borrowing against the vested portion of their deferred benefit. A note of caution should be exercised here that this borrowing should be for emergencies only. The deferred trust should not be allowed to become a "souped up" credit union. Nevertheless, this loan provision, where incorporated into the design features of the plan can, and does, in practice, serve a very useful purpose for both employee and employer alike. The pension plan mechanism does not provide for such a loan capability.

6. While pension plans frequently are "integrated" with Social Security benefits, deferred profit sharing plans never are. This could mean a plus for deferred profit sharing, but not necessarily so. It would depend entirely on the formulas involved and how they compare.

So much for the advantages; now let us look at some *disadvantages:*

1. Because of the more liberal vesting, and a general attitude that this is "employees' money" that is being invested, rather than the "employer's money," I think there is a tendency on the part of trustees to be somewhat more conservative in their investment policies than they would tend

to be in the case of a pension plan. In a pension plan, their investment policies need not be geared to short-term termination or liquidity considerations, whereas in a profit sharing plan with terminations occurring on a regular basis throughout any given year, distributions from the trust are being made continuously. What is distributed at any point of time to a given terminated employee will depend on the stock market conditions at the time of termination. If the market happens to be depressed, Joe Doaks could receive a diminished distribution from the trust, in many cases less than he might have received three to six months earlier, or for that matter, might have received six months later in a market recovery. For such an individual, at such times a deferred profit sharing trust has somehow "let him down," by not protecting his money. Never doubt that you will have such distributions and such employee attitudes!

2. In addition to the phenomenon that the distribution from a profit sharing trust is the market value of a fluctuating portfolio valuation at a given amount of time, there is a very major deterrent to deferred profit sharing plans as opposed to pension plans. A pension plan prescribes a fixed retirement benefit to which a given employee looks throughout his career. He knows what this benefit will be in dollars. (He may not necessarily know what these dollars may buy him in inflationary terms.) With a deferred profit sharing plan, however, he will never have a really comfortable assurance of what dollars he will have to retire on. He might see some encouraging charts and projections in his employee manual, but these could easily prove deceptive and either the company profit sharing contribution may not have *averaged* 6% per year over his life cycle, as the chart showed, or the earnings of the trust itself did not average 7½% per annum, as the chart showed, or if all these things did happen, he could have chosen a market slump to retire in and suddenly this accumulated profit sharing account balance, instead of being $100,000, as the chart suggested and the last statement from the trustee showed, is now a distribution from the trustee that because of current market conditions may be far less than this. Do you think he feels cheated? You bet he does! And how can this be avoided? We have pointed out so many advantages to deferred profit sharing plans, are they to be wiped out by this one overriding and damning feature?

In earlier chapters, we have indicated that with the rise of social security benefits, not in absolute dollars but in relativity to total retirement benefits, it seemed likely that the day of the formal private sector pension plan was headed for a back seat and perhaps even ultimate extinction. Surely, but for the major drawback of lack of fixed benefit on retirement, the deferred profit sharing trust might well be a more useful mechanism than the fixed private pension plan in the days ahead. This is certainly my personal view. But the dilemma remains as to how to correct the defect we have just pointed out, namely, the absence of assurance that a planned pension benefit will materialize upon retirement via the deferred profit sharing route.

Let us go back and ask ourselves, "What exactly is our *objective* in this whole retirement field?" Is it not to ensure that employees who retire from the productive main stream of corporate life, after a suitable life cycle, may do so on a reasonable economic basis that is equated with the standard of living that they have attained through the fruits of their efforts and skills over their productive life cycle? Social Security payments, which is the public sector of pension benefit to which the employee contributes through life and to which each of his employers in turn also equally contribute, forms the cornerstone of this benefit. On top of this, the private sector, whether it be through fixed benefit pension plan, or variable benefit deferred profit sharing plan, must make up the difference, to the extent such difference continues to exist in tomorrow's world. With fixed benefit pension plans, we have seen how this mechanism works. With variable benefit deferred profit sharing, we have yet to resolve how the same benefit can be assured. It seems to me that the simplest way is merely to assume the benefit. Like all forms of negotiation where the interests of the parties must somehow be accommodated, why not let the corporation have the advantages of its variable benefit deferred profit sharing plan, so it can do the following:

1. Retain variability.
2. Protect itself against adverse years.
3. Stimulate productivity through incentive.

But, to protect the employee, let the corporation *guarantee* to him that his deferred profit sharing trust will in fact yield the higher of its incentive benefit or a minimum formula pension benefit by the time he retires from the plan. This means a profit sharing plan with a pension formula umbrella. This means, in simplistic jargon, that each employee must pay for his own retirement benefit, to the extent that it exceeds Social Security payments, out of his accumulated profit sharing earnings from the company. If his profit sharing earnings are higher, he takes the higher earnings; to the extent his profit sharing earnings are deficient, the corporation has to make up the difference. This is "pay as you go" retirement philosophy. But is it really any different, no matter what you call it? Are not all benefits really a form of "pay as you go" benefits? They all come out of corporate profits, and without such profits, no benefit structure, however sophisticated nor with whatever formulas, will long endure.

Technically, this type of plan, or pension plan umbrella over a deferred profit sharing trust, which uses Social Security as a "feeder," is not recognized or sanctioned by the IRS at this time. This phenomenon eludes me if the rationale of the mechanism serves a useful purpose in retirement planning for both the employer and employee alike. I am told that the specifications of such a plan do not meet the "technical requirements of a proper pension plan." However, in spite of my years of financial experience in a variety of corporate enterprises, I cannot yet overcome a basic naiveté that presumes that if something can be shown to be constructive and useful for the benefit of all parties, then its approval into the accepted protocols of benefit plans will be eventually recognized and permitted, technical criteria notwithstanding.

Pension plans, as they have been traditionally conceived of in employee motivation, are "defensive" in character. I have tried to show that profit sharing plans, on the other hand, may well be "offensive" mechanisms, motivating employees toward the constructive improvement of productivity, and corporate profits, to their own personal benefit as well. How would you respond, as an employee, if your company told you the following:

1. We will put aside 7% of your pay into a deferred trust to take care of you when you retire. If you do not stay with us, but leave prematurely, you will, of course, not get this money. Instead, it will be turned over to your fellow employee, the one who remains with the company.

2. We will put aside a sum of money, depending on a formula of corporate earnings, into a deferred trust for your account. If the company does well, this sum of money might be 7%, 10%, maybe even 15%. It all depends on how well the company does in profits. Conversely, if the company does not fare well in a given year, or even in a period of years, reduced contributions, or perhaps even none at all, will be set aside for you. When you leave the company, you will take with you some of this money, whatever it amounts to, or perhaps even all of it. Unless you only stay for a very short while, you will take something with you in this benefit.

3. We will do what we said in item 2, but we realize that this may make you nervous if you are counting on this money to retire on. Thus, we will put a floor on this plan so that at a minimum, whether the plan 2 produces it or not, you can count on a certain formula pension benefit to be provided. If plan 2, that is, deferred profit sharing, plus Social Security, falls short, the company will establish a third fund, a pension fund to make up the difference. If fund 2 is larger than this formula pension fund, you gain, because you have earned the larger amount. If, however, fund 2 falls short, you have at least fund 3 to fall back on.

If profits are good and as planned, then, fund 2 carries the day. In this case, the "pension umbrella" promised by item 3 has cost the company *nothing*. If

Chart 40. Example of Variable Profit Sharing with Pension Umbrella *

	Case A; Profit Improvement of 10% Per Year			Case B; Profits Erratic with Declining Slump			
	Variable Profit Sharing ($)	Fixed Pension ($)	Variable with Pension Umbrella (Umbrella Additional) ($)	Pretax Profits Versus Base Year (%)	Variable Profit Sharing ($)	Fixed Pension ($)	Variable with Pension Umbrella (Umbrella Additional) ($)
Year 1	668,000	630,000		100	668,000	630,000	0
Cumulative	668,000	630,000	0		668,000	630,000	0
Year 2	724,000	630,000		110	724,000	630,000	0
Cumulative	1,392,000	1,260,000	0		1,392,000	1,260,000	0
Year 3	786,000	630,000		90	476,000	630,000	
Cumulative	2,178,000	1,890,000	0		1,868,000	1,890,000	22,000
Year 4	854,000	630,000		70	235,000	630,000	
Cumulative	3,032,000	2,520,000	0		2,103,000	2,520,000	395,000
Year 5	929,000	630,000		90	403,000	630,000	
Cumulative	3,961,000	3,150,000	0		2,506,000	3,150,000	227,000

* Based on XYZ Company with $5,000,000 pretax profits and fixed pension commitment equivalent to 7% of covered compensation.

131

fund 3 must be utilized, the company is where it would have been anyway in a formal pension plan situation, but it has had the advantage of flexibility in individual years, which possibly may have been helpful from a cash as well as earnings per share standpoint. In this plan, the good years help pay for the bad years, which is quite a constructive corporate strategy.

Again, I must point out that while I have designed such a plan many years ago and even had it approved by the IRS, in more recent years others who have tried to follow the same route have been unsuccessful on the grounds that such a pension program does not fulfill the "technical requirements of a pension plan." I repeat that this logic eludes me.

Let us consider in Chart 40 how such a plan might work.

I have said in an earlier chapter that as with most authors I have a subjective axe to grind. My axe is obviously my interest in this concept as a viable and constructive approach to pension planning in the years ahead where the public sector assumes more of the role for an employee's retirement, where the interest in portability and nonforfeiture of benefits is of paramount concern to Congress and the public, and where corporate management's interest in increased profits, through increased productivity, to pay for the rising costs of pension plans, can also be served, not to the detriment of, but to the potential supplemental benefit of, the employee himself. If, as I have suggested, private pension plans may well be headed for obsolescence, then it is not enough to allow a vacuum to come into being in the private sector.

If, as I have also suggested, man's cost of depreciation is rising in itself at the same time as man is tending to become more exposed to obsolescence, then can financial managers allow their corporations to abdicate the control of such rising costs increasingly to the public sector?

In both instances, I feel the role of the deferred profit sharing plan, with a "pension formula" umbrella, fairly designed and adequately communicated, may well provide a positive response on the part of the corporate institution to these challenges.

CHAPTER 13

WHITHER AWAY, BENEFIT PLANS?

How does one summarize the thoughts he has had on the financial considerations on Man's trend through life. I have tried to point out that man is in a state of change. He has become increasingly aware of his economics in a world dominated by today's industrial society. While abused at first, man, through the social evolution of the past 50 years or so, whether through increased social consciousness and concern for his evolving needs, through the militant proddings of unionism, or whatever, man has become increasingly aware that basic wage alone is not enough and will not sustain him throughout his economic life cycle and his residual mortality cycle beyond. We have examined in this book the environment of the "onward and upward" society that has characterized the past generation. We have yet to speculate on what will characterize the generations that lie ahead of man.

We have also posed the observation that man is a depreciating asset of our modern industrial environment, and as such, he is susceptible to the phenomena that are characteristic of other corporate assets, namely depreciation, obsolescence, and in Man's case, transience.

We have tried in this book to explore not only the accounting problems of reconciling these phenomena, but also, much more importantly, the financial implications of these developments and the financial dialogues that they raise as they emerge in importance to our corporate scene and as they bode for future importance in the projections of tomorrow's profile for the industrial enterprise itself.

We can see that the ante for the cost of supporting man is rising persistantly, even to the extent that someday we may not be able to afford the luxury of such an asset. We have discussed the trend toward earlier retirement of man whereby he can earlier enjoy the fruits of the productivity advances of the industrial society and retire at a progressively younger age, a dubious association with the drone society that our present psychology proclaims as the future objective to which our working force aspires.

All of the sociological elements we have tried to recognize and examine to the extent presently reasonably possible. No one can read this book without realizing at a minimum that man's costs are rising at a rapid pace, with fringe benefits rising as rapidly or even more so than basic wage alone, as we press forward in pursuit of this "onward and upward" society.

But no book that attempts to chronicle the present in such a perspective can be considered complete until it addresses itself also to the question, "Where do we go from here?" What is the role of fringe benefits in tomorrow's industrial environment?

Surely the mood of the industrial working society will best be paraphrased by the phrase, "But what are you doing for me now?" Can you doubt this in today's world where we look increasingly to the political entity to resolve and ensure against all but the inert variables among the economic elements that confront man's cradle to grave economic path through life?

Can anyone doubt that the trend for increasing and more diverse benefits for man lie yet along the path ahead? And what could such benefits be?

1. Shorter work week.
2. Longer vacations.
3. More holidays.
4. Guaranteed annual wage.
5. Optional overtime (this exists in the option of working if you want to, not when your corporation needs you).
6. Earlier retirement, at no reduction of retirement pay of course.
7. Post retirement protection against the impact of future inflation, that is, cost of living escalators.
8. Retirement counseling prior to retirement to psychologically prepare for it.
9. Investment counseling for the individual so that his retirement finances are geared to his most effective individual needs.
10. More benefits for employees paid for by the corporation, that is

    Legal services.
    Travel services.
    Cooperative working services, for example, "I can get it for you wholesale, why pay retail?"

I conclude from these items that there are definitely more benefits and more costs to come.

And how will the industrial enterprise withstand this onslaught? How can the financial executive protect his corporation in this environment?

The crystal ball becomes cloudy at this point as you would cynically expect of any view of the future, but let us look for guidance in the soil of the present.

What does the financial executive do now in the face of rising labor costs to protect his corporation? Increase sales prices? Definitely he should do so, but also he should explore increased productivity that might serve to reduce *per unit* labor costs in the face of increased aggregate labor dollar increases. As applied to fringe benefits, this implies a scrutiny of the efficiency of the fringe benefit package itself. Are our fringe benefits, however, socially oriented and efficient? This is a highly important and most interesting question which I raise in this final chapter. Taken individually, who could possibly fault the social desirability of any individual benefit? Obviously no one. However, consider the following:

Does the working single girl in her early twenties care for a pension benefit at age 65 for herself?

Does the single person, whether male or female, need a death benefit?

Does the probably younger transient care much for a longer term benefit that he will forfeit when he leaves?

Does the older employee want a maternity benefit that he or she will not use?

With increasing double incomes of working husbands and wives, do they care for a nominal group life death benefit?

This is only a start to the serious questions that could be raised about the legitimacy or efficiency of some of our more accepted modern day benefit programs. Each in itself is a valid benefit—desirable for some, but of no value definitely to other employees who work side by side just as diligently as those who derive primary benefit. Upon inspection of this thesis, I am sure that you will find that at any point in time, we are spending considerable sums of the corporate enterprise funds on benefits for certain employees who have no use for, and will not reasonably derive any benefits from, such expenditures. From an insurance standpoint, this seems appropriate, because insurance rates and profits are derived from an expectation that this very inefficiency will in fact exist. From the financial executive's point of view, this represents a form of inefficiency that seems terribly wasteful. When benefits themselves are so expensive and are increasing in cost enormously over the years, a corporation has got to have its head examined to keep paying tribute to an inefficient system that capitalizes on unproductivity. This is surely sacrilege!

But what imaginatively can be done about it? As long as the debits of corporate expenditure are charged off to earnings per share and are accepted, is any challenge to this form of efficiency possible or even likely?

The insurance industry will finally point out, and with some legitimacy, that rates quoted for various benefits are in themselves predicated on total group participation, which is another way of announcing that they expect and count on the basic inefficiency of the plan. That is not their concern. But it *is* the concern of the financial executive.

Is it inconceivable that a corporation might not pool its benefit costs into one reservoir of purchasing power from which a "shopping list" of benefits might be selected by individual employees, as his or her needs require, at a given moment in the employee life cycle? Employees would not receive an arbitrary benefit structure tailored for the entire group profile, but select rather, the lesser profile that more pertinently fits the individual's immediate needs. If a given "pocket book" were provided for such a purpose, why not let employees spend it as *they* see fit, not as *we* or our insurance advisers and consultants see fit. As long as the "pocket book" is the same, why should the corporation itself care how it is spent? On the contrary, it is in the corporation's interest that such funds are directed as efficiently as possible to the immediate and most pressing needs of its current roster of employees. With a fixed pocket book for such a program, what is the better employee morale mechanism? I would vote for employee selectivity and less of a dogmatic structure into which we try to fit our majority employee needs.

I suspect that this is a rather idealistic and simplistic view. I am aware of the legitmate contention that present insurance rates relate directly to "the law of averages," and if you disturb such a balance, you throw into "a cocked hat" your present structure of quoted insurance rates. And yet, is this reason enough for capitlizing on inefficiency, for continuing to provide benefits for employees that few require, or even that many require but only over a different span in their life cycle? A variable fringe benefit package, constantly changing to be responsive to the needs of the employees for whom it is dedicated, is without doubt a rewarding, even if idealistic objective. It deserves the application of far more imaginative thought process on the part of the corporation's financial executive and the fringe benefit professional community which serves him than it is receiving at this time.

Those financial executives who have experienced what are called "retrospective rating plans" are well aware that in the insurance field, as a general long-term principle, "you pay for what you get." It is only a matter of timing. This is not true, perhaps, of casualty insurance, where it should be obvious that not every company has a major fire disaster in its corporate career. But in medical insurance, unless, like a gypsy, you flit from carrier to carrier, which will not endear you to the insurance community, you will pay for what you get without question. The same is true in larger group life, accident, and disability policies, and even workmen's compensation.

If you accept this hypothesis, and I believe you should, then it is not hard for you to accept the hypothesis that larger companies are paying for their fringe benefits as they are, in fact, utilized by their employees. The curve is smoothed somewhat by the carrier. The extremes are leveled down; the administration, litigation, negotiation of claim, and such, are transferred to independent professionals, but you have paid for what your employees got. If this is so, then why not let the employees select what they want from a shopping list? You will still only pay for what they get, but you will have, perhaps, happier employees.

It is not my wish to be deceptive or simplistic in this final chapter; therefore, I am only urging that an imaginative thought process take place on this suggestion. It could well be that this device might lead to higher costs, not just higher initial premiums, as it would at the outset. But under retrospective rating, it may well be that the costs in time will not be significantly different, only more efficiently deployed.

If this were to be proven to be true, then it surely would be worth it.

And how might such a wild scheme be funded? Why not profit sharing? Why not a formula pool based on corporate earnings, which could create a fund for each employee out of which he could shop for his benefits as his present condition and needs required, electing cash or deferred compensation for the difference, if any. This sounds just great, but it has two big drawbacks:

1. What happens when profits go down? No fringe benefits?
2. What happens to the short-sighted employee who underestimates his need for benefits and elects to take his share in compensation instead?

Both of these are valid obstacles. Both would certainly need to be resolved before any such plan could be remotely considered feasible. Probably some form of banking of an accrued benefits pool, prior to committing a shopping list would be required, so that the employee always has some uncommitted reserve available to tide him over come the rainy day. Perhaps even this is not enough and there must also be a "floor commitment" on the part of the corporation so that even when the employee's bank of accrued benefits is exhausted, a certain minimum benefit structure will be maintained by the corporation.

You may well ask, "Why is all this really necessary?"

Who knows where tomorrow's benefit trails lead? One thing we can assume is that they lead to change. Reflect only for a moment on the dynamics of benefit plan development over the past generation. What financial executive can fail to recognize the major impact that these changes have made on the cost structure of his company, particularly if it happens to be labor intensive. No longer can he afford to consider the labor cost alone of new employees added incrementally to his economic projections. He must also tack on the fringe benefit cost package which in all likelihood will run 25 to 30% additional premium on the labor dollar in today's industrial world. Today's benefit planner also knows that benefit plans themselves are far from static programs. They are in a constant state of change, edit, modification, requotation, new carriers, new experience histories, new demands for improvement, new needs, and such.

Can there be anyone who believes that this evolutionary process of change will not continue at least apace into tomorrow's industrial future? Of course it will.

Then how does tomorrow's financial executive plan for the identification and proper measurement of such future costs as they occur? More importantly, how can he counsel his management on the optimum financial strategies to cope with the economic demands that tomorrow's benefit plans will surely make on the pocketbook of corporate earnings per share?

Increasing automation to lessen the exposure to people cost? This surely is one avenue. Multinationalism? Escape to less developed countries where this trend is less far advanced? Again, this is a possibility, but at best a temporary one, and one beset with additional perils.

What else is there? Where else to turn? There are no obvious answers. The financial executive must use imagination to conceive of new unconventional concepts not now in his financial manuals, perhaps not now even in obscure counsel of any sort.

A larger use of the profit sharing concept might be one of these possible approaches, as this chapter has suggested.

There surely are others to be explored, but the objective of any new device to fringe benefit strategy must be the same—to somehow lower the unit cost of man to the economic enterprise that uses him. Every financial executive knows that the propensity of operating people in his organization is to spend, to think up new programs, additive programs to extend immediate activities outward in a fashion imitative of the expanding nature of our very universe. If this is the psychology under which the modern industrial corporation works, then the pressures for cost increases, both laterally and vertically, must be enormous. Only by pruning away at the same time what is no longer needed, what is inefficient, what is unproductive, can we possibly hope to contain this cost explosion tendency in an "onward and upward" society. Such a pruning process is not a natural corollary to planning for growth. This, then, is the cross that the financial executive, perhaps even alone in the organization, must bear; he must be the guardian of the pruning shears. He is "Old Mr. Budgetary Controls"; he is "Old Mr. Bodies-Out-The-Door." And, in the context of this book on fringe benefits, he must play the devil's advocate as to what can be pruned away, or taken away in trade-offs, what can be turned from a fixed rising cost to at least a flexible cost variable with corporate profits. This, then, is a fitting note on which to end this book—on a note of challenge to the financial executive to seek out imaginative solutions to the rising cost of man and his fringe benefits. The success with which financial executives will meet this challenge may decide whether the future industrial enterprise of tomorrow can afford the peculiar asset we call Man.

APPENDIX A. SAMPLE DEFERRED PROFIT SHARING PLAN

XYZ Corporation
Plan of Profit Sharing

PREAMBLE

XYZ Corporation, to recognize the contributions made to its operations by its employees, and to reward such contributions by means of a plan of sharing profits, and to provide additional incentive for employees to remain with the company and to increase their efforts for its success, and to provide additional security for employees on their retirement, has established this plan of profit sharing (hereinafter called "the Plan"). The Plan shall be administered by a committee (hereinafter called the "Committee"), and funded by means of a trust fund created by XYZ Corporation (hereinafter called the "Trust") pursuant to a separate trust agreement entered into with a trustee (hereinafter called the "Trustee").

I. MEMBERSHIP

1.(a) Every person in the full-time employ of the Company [as defined in subparagraph (d) below] on the first business day of any calendar year (hereinafter called the "eligibility date"), who continues in the full-time employ of the Company throughout such calendar year, shall be deemed a member of the Plan for such year. Persons whose customary employment is for less than 30 hours in any one week shall not be considered employed full-time.

(b) In cases of persons employed before January 1, 1968, if they were in the Company's employ continuously from May 1, 1967 until December 31, 1967, they shall be deemed to have been members of the Plan for the short period ending on such date, but for fiscal years ending on or before April 30, 1967, persons employed after April 16, 1953 were not eligible for membership before the fiscal year following their completion with the Company of two years continuous employment.

(c) Any person who is in the Company's employ at the end of any calendar year, but who was employed at the beginning of such year or at any time during such year (i) by XYZ Corporation, or (ii) by any other corporation at least 50% of whose voting stock is owned by XYZ Corporation (hereinafter called an "XYZ affiliate"), or (iii) by any corporation at least 50% of whose voting stock is owned by an XYZ affiliate (hereinafter called an "XYZ subaffiliate") or by another XYZ subaffiliate, shall be deemed a member of the Plan for such year, provided that such person was continuously employed full-time by one or more of such corporations during all of such year. However, the allocation to such person of a portion of the contribution to the Trust by the Company in respect of such year shall be based solely upon the compensation paid to such person by the Company for that year, and whenever the compensation paid to such person for such year shall be material for any purpose of this Plan, only the compensation paid by the Company shall be counted.

(d) Wherever the term "Company" is used in this Plan, it shall mean XYZ Corporation, a New York corporation, for all periods ending on or before December 5, 1969, shall mean XYZ Corporation, a New York corporation, for all periods ending after December 5, 1969, and shall mean any affiliated corporation, subsidiary, and any other corporation which, with the consent of the Board of Directors of XYZ Company, adopts this Plan as an employer hereunder. A Company which has duly adopted the Plan is sometimes hereinafter referred to as a "Participating Company." Wherever the name "XYZ Corporation" is used in this Plan, except in this subparagraph, it shall mean the Delaware corporation of that name which is the parent of the XYZ Corporation.

2. Notwithstanding anything hereinabove contained in paragraph 1 of this Article, no person employed by the Company shall be deemed a member of this Plan for any year in which he shall be covered as a participant under a plan providing pensions or other retirement benefits to which the Company is obligated to make a contribution (whether or not such plan is covered by a collective bargaining agreement), other than (i) a pension, profit sharing, stock bonus or other plan established by the Company exclusively for its own employees or for the employees of corporations under common control with the Company, or (ii) the national social security plan, or (iii) any other public plan established by federal, state or local law.

3. Any time spent in the armed forces of the United States of America following immediately upon time spent in the service of the Company by an employee of the Company who is received back into the service of the Company within 90 days after the date of his discharge from the armed forces, or such

additional period during which his rights are protected by law, shall count as employment by the Company for the purpose of paragraph 1 above and in determining length of membership in this Plan; provided, however, that no part of the Company contribution for any year shall be allocated under Article III to an employee who is in the armed forces during any part of such year, unless he has returned to the service of the Company on or before the last day of such year.

4. Except as provided in paragraphs 1 and 3 above, and 7 below, a former employee upon reemployment after termination of employment shall be deemed a new employee for the purpose of qualifying as an eligible employee, and no credit for the prior employment shall be allowed in computing the eligibility period.

5. Any interruption in employment not exceeding two continuous years, which is recognized by the Committee as a leave of absence under criteria uniformly applied by the Committee, shall be deemed as not terminating or interrupting continuous employment. Leaves of absence may be recognized for such purposes as, but shall not necessarily be limited to, education and training, sickness, accident, disability, military duty, public service and lay-offs.

6. The Company shall give written notice to every employee of the Company, as he shall become a member for the first time, of the existence of this Plan and of said employee's participation therein, and said notice shall also set forth the basic provisions of this Plan, or, in lieu thereof, be accompanied by a copy of this instrument.

II. CONTRIBUTIONS

1. On or before the last day of each fiscal year the Board of Directors of each Participating Company shall, in its sole discretion, determine an amount or the percentage of current and accumulated profits which shall constitute its Profit Sharing Pool for purposes of this Plan.

2. That portion of the Profit Sharing Pool which does not exceed 7½% of the aggregate Compensation of the members of such Participating Company shall be known as the Basic Contribution of such Participating Company and shall be paid to the Trustee and allocated to the accounts of the members of such Participating Company in accordance with the provisions of Article III, paragraph 2. The balance of the Profit Sharing Pool, if any, shall be known as the Variable Contribution of such Participating Company and shall be paid to the Trustee and allocated to the accounts of the members of such Participating Company, subject to the provisions of Article III, paragraph 3.

3. Notwithstanding the foregoing provisions of this Article, the total Basic

and Variable Contribution paid into the Trust by a Participating Company with respect to any fiscal year shall in no event exceed 15% of the aggregate compensation of the members employed by such Participating Company in the year with respect to which such contribution is made.

4. Each Participating Company shall pay its share of the expenses of the Trust, including reasonable Trustees' fees, as shall be determined by the Committee. In the event that a Participating Company does not pay such expenses directly, the Trustee shall charge the same to that portion of the Trust assets allocable to the members employed by such Participating Company.

5. For purposes of this Plan, "current profits" of a Participating Company means such Company's profits for the fiscal year in respect of which a contribution is made and "accumulated profits" means aggregate net profits and losses for all years and periods of such Participating Company ending on the last day of the fiscal year or period in respect of which a contribution is made. The amount of a Participating Company's current and accumulated profits as determined in accordance with good accounting practice, consistently applied and approved by the Board of Directors, shall be binding and conclusive upon such Company, the Trustee, and all members.

6.(a) Each member may elect to make personal contributions to the Trust in an amount up to 10% (as he shall designate) of his Compensation (as defined in Article III, paragraph 5). Such personal contributions shall be made by payroll deductions equal to 2, 4, 6, 8, or 10% (as the member shall designate) of the weekly or monthly wage, as the case may be, authorized by a written direction of the member in such form as may be prescribed by the Committee, to be first effective for the pay day ending with or directly preceding a quarterly valuation date, provided that such direction shall be delivered to the Committee at least 20 calendar days before such pay day.

(b) A member may, within the limitations prescribed above, elect to increase, decrease or discontinue his personal contributions at any time on written notice, in such form as may be prescribed by the Committee, delivered to it at least 20 calendar days before the effective pay day, which shall be a pay day ending with or directly preceding a quarterly valuation date.

(c) A member may elect to withdraw all or part of his personal contributions as of the quarterly valuation date next following such election by written notice in such form as may be prescribed by the Committee, delivered to it at least 20 calendar days before such valuation date. A member may not resume personal contributions prior to the expiration of six months following the effective date of any such election to withdraw (in whole or in part) his personal contributions.

(d) Any such election (i) to increase, decrease or discontinue, and (ii) to withdraw (in whole or in part), personal contributions may not be made more often than once during each year.

(e) The aggregate amount of all personal contributions deducted by the Company in any month shall be paid to the Trust by the Company not later than the last business day of the next succeeding month.

III. ALLOCATION OF CONTRIBUTIONS
AND MEMBERS' ACCOUNTS

1. The Trustee shall set up a separate Part A Account and a Part B Account for each member who participates in the Plan.

2. The Basic Contribution of each Participating Company shall be allocated by the Trustee as directed by the Committee among the Part A Accounts of members employed by the Participating Company on the basis of their respective amounts of Compensation from such Company, so that the amount allocated to each such member's account shall be that portion of such contribution which the member's Compensation from such Company for that year bears to the aggregate Compensation from such Company of all such members employed by such Company for that year.

3. The portion of the Variable Contribution, if any, of each Participating Company to be paid to the Trustee and allocated to the Part B Accounts of the members of such Participating Company shall be determined in accordance with the following procedure:

(a) The amount of a member's share in the Variable Contribution of the Participating Company by which he is employed shall be that portion of the Variable Contribution which his Compensation for the year bears to the aggregate Compensation of all members of the Participating Company for that year.

(b) Before July 1 of each year each member may elect, by written notice in such form as may be prescribed by the Committee, to have 0, 25, 50, 75, or 100% of his share of the Variable Contribution paid to the Trustee and allocated to his Part B Account. The portion of the Variable Contribution which the member elects not to have paid to the Trustee shall be paid to him in cash as soon as is feasible after the amount of his share of the Variable Contribution has been determined.

(c) Notwithstanding the foregoing, if in any fiscal year the Committee shall determine that the elections by members employed by a Participating Company with respect to the Variable Contribution shall cause the Plan to fail to satisfy the requirements of Revenue Ruling 56-497 (or any subsequent ruling of similar purpose), the Committee shall reduce the amount of the Variable Contribution payable to the Trust for such fiscal year on behalf of the members employed by that Participating Company who are among the one-third highest paid such members by proportionately reducing each election to have a share paid to the Trustee under subparagraph (b) above to the extent necessary to meet the requirements of such Revenue Ruling.

(d) If, after the foregoing computations have been made, the aggregate of the Company's basic and Variable Contributions shall exceed the limitations set forth in Article II, paragraph 3, then the Committee shall reduce on a pro rata basis the share of each member in the Company's Variable Contribution to the extent necessary to come within such limit.

4. The amount of each member's personal contribution under Article II, paragraph 6, shall be allocated to his Part B Account.

5. In computing contributions and amounts to be allocated to members, the Committee shall apply the following rules:

(a) "Compensation" shall mean the amounts paid for services rendered, and shall include all salary, commissions, bonuses, and overtime, but shall not include cash profit sharing payments, credits and benefits under this plan, or amounts contributed by the Company to any employee pension, welfare or health insurance plan.

(b) A former member whose employment was terminated by reason of retirement, disability, or death during the year as described in paragraphs 1, 2, or 4 of Article V shall participate in the Company's contribution for the year in which employment so terminated on the basis of his compensation.

(c) A member who is discharged or resigns shall not participate in the Company's contribution for the year in which his employment so terminated.

IV. INVESTMENT OF FUNDS

1. All funds allocated to members' Part A Account shall be held as a single fund (hereinafter called the "General Fund"), and the Trustee shall not invest separately the members' several accounts. The General Fund shall be invested by the Trustee in any property of any kind, in accordance with the provisions of the separate trust agreement entered into with the Trustee.

2. Each member will elect, in accordance with rules prescribed by the Committee, that contributions to his Part B Account shall be invested in one of the following Funds:

(a) *Fixed Income Fund.* The "Fixed Income Fund" shall consist of investments, selected for the primary purpose of protection of principal and reasonable income yield, in any property, real or personal, or part interest therein, wherever situate, including, but without being limited to, governmental, corporate or personal obligations, trust and participation certificates, leaseholds, fee titles, mortgages and other interests in realty, preferred stocks, mutual funds, and any other evidences of indebtedness or ownership on a fixed income basis, excluding property, stock, or securities of the Company, common stocks, and any other similar equity investment.

(b) *Equity Fund*. The "Equity Fund" shall consist of equity investments selected for the primary purpose of capital appreciation, including investments in common or preferred stocks, convertible bonds, and any other form of equity investment.

(c) *Diversified Fund*. The "Diversified Fund" shall consist of investments selected for the primary purpose of achieving a balance among protection of principal, income yield, and capital appreciation, including properties of the kind prescribed for the Fixed Income Fund and the Equity Fund.

There may be included as an investment of any of the foregoing Funds any trust or trust fund, of which the Trustee is also the trustee, which has been qualified under Section 401(a) and is exempt under Section 501(a) of the Internal Revenue Code of 1954, maintained by the Trustee as a medium for the collective investment of funds of pension, profit sharing or other employee benefit trusts, the provisions of which are not inconsistent with the provisions of this Trust Agreement or the purposes of the particular Fund, and the provisions of any such trust shall be deemed a part of this Agreement.

The election or modification of one of the foregoing options shall be made in accordance with rules prescribed by the Committee.

3. The Committee shall cause the Trustee to ascertain the market value of members' Part A Accounts and Part B Accounts quarterly. The member accounts shall be adjusted as of the last day of the fiscal year (before allocation of the Company's contribution for the year) to reflect the proportionate beneficial interest of each member in income collected or accrued by the Trust, realized and unrealized profits and losses, expenses, forfeitures, and other transactions affecting each respective account. Such adjustments shall also be made as of the last day of any other quarter with respect to the accounts of members who have terminated during the quarter. For purposes of such adjustments, forfeitures occurring during any year shall be allocated to the Part A Account of members employed on December 31st of such year in the same proportions provided in paragraph 2 of Article III for the allocation of the Company's contributions in respect of such year.

4. Notwithstanding any other provision of this Plan, the Committee may appoint one or more investment counselors with full power, discretion, control and authority to select the investments for the Funds described in this Article and to buy, sell and trade in stocks, bonds and other securities and assets for the Trustees and in the Trustees' name or in the name of a nominee, without independent investigation, or exercise of discretion, by the Trustrees. The Committee shall require investment counsel to furnish such periodic and other reports to the Trustees as it deems to be in the best interests of the Trust. The

Trustees shall not be liable to the Company, or to any employee or to any beneficiary of an employee, for any loss whatsoever attributable to an appointment of investment counsel under this paragraph.

5. The fact that allocations of the Company's contributions shall be made and credited to the account of a member shall not vest any right, title or interest in such assets in such member except at the time or times and upon the terms and conditions herein provided. No member or exmember or other Company employee shall have any legal or equitable rights in the assets of the Trust from time to time, except as provided in this Plan.

6. In the event that any other plan is made a part of and consolidated and merged with this Plan, all of the assets and accounts of the trust created incident to that plan, together with all amounts segregated for deferred payment to participants or beneficiaries of participants under said plan, shall be administered under the terms applicable to Part A Accounts under this Plan. The rights and interests of the participants under said other plan and trust, and the manner in which the trust assets shall be paid out and distributed, shall thereafter be determined exclusively in accordance with the terms and provisions of this Plan and the Trust incident hereto. In no event, however, shall a participant of the plan and trust that has been made a part of and consolidated and merged with this Plan and the Trust incident hereto have a vested interest in his benefits attributed to such merged plan and the trust of less than that to which he was entitled as of the effective date of said consolidation and merger of the plans and trusts, and the Committee shall certify to the Trustee the vested interest of each participant in such plan and trust.

V. DISTRIBUTION OF BENEFITS

1. A member shall be entitled to retire on December 31 following his attaining the age of sixty (60) years, but he may continue in active service of the Company beyond the age of (60), with the Company's approval, and as a fully participating member of this Plan. Upon retirement the entire amount in the member's Part A Account and Part B Account on the valuation date coinciding with or next following retirement and the amount, if any, to which he may be entitled under paragraph 5(b) of Article III shall be paid to him in cash or in kind by one or more of the following methods, as the Committee may determine in its absolute discretion: (1) in a lump sum payable (together with such interest as may have been actually earned thereon if the member's account is segregated as hereinbelow provided) at such time within one year after the end of the fiscal

year of retirement as the chief executive officer of the Company shall direct; or (2) in not more than 15 annual installments, the first installment being payable (with interest as above) within said one-year period and the remaining installments being held in a separate account on the terms hereinafter provided and paid to the member together with increments, if any, on such unpaid installments; or (3) by the purchase and delivery to the member of nontransferable annuity contract on his life; or (4) in any other manner. Pending the determination of the Committee as to the method of payment, the member's account shall be held in a separate account on the following terms. Separate accounts shall be segregated from the General Fund, the Fixed Income Fund, the Equity Fund, and the Diversified Fund, and invested only in United States government bonds or deposited in savings banks, unless the retiring member shall direct the Committee in writing to leave his accounts in such Funds provided, however, that when an optional method of settlement is selected, the present value of the payments to be made to the participant shall be more than 50% of the present value of the total payments to be made to the participant and his beneficiaries.

2. A member shall be deemed to have retired from service, and shall accordingly be entitled to the benefits stated in paragraph 1 above, on December 31st of any year in which in the opinion of a doctor selected by the Committee (which opinion shall be conclusive for purposes of this Plan) he shall have become totally and permanently disabled. Total and permanent disability shall mean the complete inability of a member to perform any and every duty of any gainful occupation with the Company for which he is reasonably fitted by training, education, or experience.

3.(a) In case of the discharge or resignation of a member prior to retirement, other than for the causes stated in paragraphs 5 and 6 below, the member's benefits under this Plan shall be limited to the vested part of the value of the member's accounts on the valuation date coinciding with or next following such discharge or resignation (hereinafter called "the vested equity"). Such vested equity shall consist of

(i) The aggregate value credited to his Part B Account, plus

(ii) That portion of the balance of the value of the member's Part A Account which on the date of such discharge or resignation shall be nonforfeitable, as described below.

The nonforfeitable portion of the member's Part A Account under (ii) above shall be determined by the number of full years of such member's continuous membership in this Plan, as follows:

Number of Full Years	Percentage (%) Nonforfeitable
1	None
2	10
3	20
4	30
5	40
6	70
7	100

(b) For this purpose, membership during the entire short period ending December 31, 1967, shall count as a full year of membership in this Plan. (Reference is made to Article I, paragraph 7, for instances in which employment by, or membership in the plan of profit sharing maintained by any of the corporations mentioned in such paragraph shall be considered as membership in this Plan.)

(c) A member's vested equity shall be paid to the member in cash or in kind by one of the methods set forth in paragraph 1 of this Article V, as the Committee may determine in its absolute discretion. Pending the determination of the Committee as to the method of payment, the member's vested equity shall be held in a separate account on the terms provided in paragraph 1 of this Article.

4.(a) In case of the death of a member while in the active employ of the Company, or of an ex-member before complete distribution of his accounts, then the amount in his accounts on the next following valuation date, plus the amount, if any, to which he may be entitled under paragraph 5(b) of Article III, or the entire undistributed balance of any separate account maintained for him, as the case may be, shall be paid forthwith in cash or in kind, as the Committee may determine in its absolute discretion, without interest or other adjustment, in a lump sum as a death benefit to the beneficiary or beneficiaries named by the member in the then most recent written designation filed with the Committee (or with the Trustee, as the case may be), or, if no designation of beneficiary is then in effect, to the spouse of the member, or, if there be none, to the direct descendants of the member, equally (per stirpes), or, if there be none, to the parents of the member equally or to the survivor between them.

(b) A member may designate the payment of his death benefits in installments, and in such case the deceased member's account shall be maintained as a separate account (if it is not already being so held), on the terms provided in paragraph 1 of this Article for separate accounts.

(c) Whenever a member to whom any payment is required to be made under this Plan cannot be located by the Trustee for a period of three years from the due date of such payment, the payment due to such member shall be paid as hereinabove provided in the eventuality of death of a member.

(d) Whenever the Trustee cannot locate any beneficiary to whom a payment is required to be made under this Plan for a period of three years from the due date of any such payment, the payment due to such beneficiary shall be paid ratably to the other beneficiary or beneficiaries named by the member, or, if there be none, the member shall be deemed to have named no beneficiary.

(e) In the event the Trustee is unable to locate any of the persons named to take a member's share under this Plan or the failure of the member to designate a beneficiary, or if there be no such persons then living, then the entire amount in the member's account shall be forfeited

5. Notwithstanding anything hereinabove to the contrary, but subject to the provisions of Article VIII, if the Company shall discharge a member for conduct detrimental to the Company, including but not limited to his dishonesty or disloyalty, or if a member shall, during or after employment, breach the terms of any agreement with the Company relating to patent assignments, shop rights, trade secrets, and the like, or if the provisions of paragraph 6 of this Article shall become operative, the member shall forfeit the entire remaining amount in his account and shall be entitled to no further benefits under this Plan, except that the member shall be entitled to his interest in his Part B Account.

6. Any member of the Plan who shall at any time engage or be employed in, or have any direct or indirect financial interest in, any occupation or business which is in competition with the Company, whether or not he is then employed by or has retired from the Company, under such circumstances that the Board of Directors of the Company shall decide that the business of the Company may be substantially and adversely affected by such competition from such member, may be notified in writing by the Company to cease such competition forthwith at penalty of forfeiting his benefits under this Plan to the extent described in paragraph 5 above. Failure on the part of such member to cease such competition within the specified time following such notice, or any extension thereof granted by the Company, shall result in such forfeiture. The decision of the Board of Directors to act in accordance with the provisions of this paragraph shall be final and binding on the Company, the Committee, the Trustee, and all members in the Plan. Nothing herein shall be deemed to affect the Company's right to discharge any employee at any time without notice.

7. The Committee shall apprise the Trustee of the occurrence of any of the contingencies provided for in paragraphs 3, 4, 5, and 6 of this Article, and any

amount standing to the accounts of any member which shall become forfeited as provided in said paragraphs shall be transferred to a suspense account for allocation to members in the manner provided in Article IV, paragraph 3.

VI. LOANS TO MEMBERS

The Committee, upon written application from a member, and upon a finding by the Committee of financial need, may permit such member to borrow an amount not to exceed 50% of the amount credited to his Part B Account, plus 50% of the vested amount allocated to his Part A Account, determined as of the latest published valuation of his accounts next preceding the application. Such financial need may include medical expenditures for the member or his family, the purchase of a home or improvements thereon, the education of a member of his family, or other significant financial need. In making its determination of eligibility for loans, the Committee shall adopt nondiscriminatory rules and apply them on a uniform basis. Loans shall be secured by the vested interest of the member under the Plan, shall be made on notes in a form approved by the Committee, shall require repayment within a specified period, and shall bear interest at the prevailing rate.

VII. ADMINISTRATION OF THE PLAN

1. XYZ Corporation shall from time to time appoint not less than three persons as members of the Committee, which shall administer this Plan as herein described. Any member of the Committee may resign at any time upon delivering to XYZ Corporation a written notice of such resignation, and any member of the Committee appointed hereunder may be removed by said corporation forthwith without cause. Said corporation may appoint a member of the Committee as a successor to any member who has resigned or been removed.

2. All Company contributions, personal contributions of members, and other assets subject to this Plan shall be held and administered as a trust fund pursuant to a trust agreement between the Company and the Trustee (hereinafter called the ''Trust Agreement''), and the Trustee shall have all powers necessary for the performance of its duties as provided in the Trust Agreement.

3. All actions of the Committee shall be by vote of a majority of the persons then serving as members of the Committee. No Committee member who is a member of the Plan shall take part in any action concerning his participation in this Plan, except insofar as his own participation may be effected by actions taken with respect to members generally. The Committee may meet informally,

or take action without the necessity of meeting as a group. Any two Committee members shall have the power to execute on behalf of the Committee all instruments required whose execution has been authorized by the Committee. The Committee shall have full power to determine any question affecting the rights of any person entilted to payment of any benefit under this Plan.

4. The Company shall advise the Committee of the occurrence of any events requiring the taking of any action by the Committee under this Plan. The Committee shall be fully protected in taking any action upon any paper or document believed by the Committee to be genuine and to have been properly signed and presented by the Company.

5. No member of the Committee shall be liable under this Plan for any act of omission or commission by the Committee in carrying out in good faith the intent and purpose of this Plan, where the Plan does not explicitly indicate the course to be taken by the Committee; and in all other cases a Committee member shall only be liable for his own fraud, misfeasance, or willful neglect.

6. The members of the Committee shall serve without compensation but shall be entitled to reimbursement from the Company for all reasonable expenses incurred by them, including fees for counsel; and the Company agrees to indemnify and save the members of the Committee harmless against any liabilities which they may incur in the exercise or their duties under this Plan.

VIII. AMENDMENT AND TERMINATION

1. The Plan, or any part thereof, is subject to change by XYZ Corporation at any time and from time to time, or may be terminated at any time by said corporation, or said corporation may suspend the making of contributions for a fixed or indeterminate period; provided, however, that no change may be made in the Plan which shall vest in the Company directly or indirectly any interest, ownership, or control in any assets of the Trust; and provided further that no change may be made which would divest a member of any interest then vested in him, except than any rights accrued or vested under that Plan may be adjusted among members by amendments made prior to securing or in order to secure the initial approval of the Plan and Trust by the Commissioner of Internal Revenue as a qualified, tax-free employee plan and trust under the Internal Revenue Code. In the event of the termination of the Plan, or in the event of a complete discontinuance of contributions to the Trust which is deemed for tax purposes to be a termination of the Plan, no new funds shall be contributed and the assets on hand shall be vested one hundred percent (100%) in favor of each member. No distribution shall be made of any amount so vested except upon the occurrence of any of the events stipulated in paragraphs 1, 2, 3, and 4 of

Article V and then only in the manner provided in said Article V.

2. In the event the Company shall cease to exist or another company shall succeed to any portion of the business of this Company, if this Plan and the Trust shall have been in force until such time, the Company's liability may be assumed by an appropriate written instrument by any successor to the business of the Company, corporate or otherwise, or to any portion of such business, or by any other business organization which employs a substantial number of the members of this Plan; or, in lieu thereof, the amounts in the accounts of any members under this Plan may be transferred to the qualified employees' trust of such successor or other company employing such members. Any members under this Plan who refuses an offer to work for such other business organization on terms at least as favorable as the terms that are then prevailing for such member with this Company shall be deemed to have severed his employment before retirement. All other members under this Plan who do not become employees of such other business organization shall be deemed to have retired.

IX. WITHDRAWAL OF A COMPANY

1. If at any time any Company included in this Plan shall cease to participate in the Plan for any reason, the Committee shall provide for the withdrawal or segregation of that Company's pro rata share of the assets in the Trust established pursuant to the Plan. The amount of such pro rata share shall be the net value of the interest in the Trust Fund of the members, former members, and beneficiaries of that Company determined as of the effective date of such withdrawal. Such determination shall be made by the Committee. The Committee shall select the assets of the Trust to be withdrawn or segregated in the amount of that Company's pro rata share so determined, and its valuation of said assets for that purpose shall be conclusive.

2. If the withdrawal of such Company from this Plan has the effect of a termination of the Plan so far as that Company and its members are concerned, then the rights of that Company's members, formers members, and beneficiaries shall be governed by the provisions of Article VIII hereof.

X. MISCELLANEOUS

1. Members are prohibited from making assignments of or subjecting their interests under this Plan to any lien.

2. Neither the establishment of this Plan, nor any modification thereof, nor

the creation of any fund, trust or account, nor the payment of any benefits, shall be construed:

(i)   As giving any member or employee of the Company the right to be retained in the service of the Company, and all members and other employees shall remain subject to discharge to the same extent as if this Plan had never been adopted; or

(ii) As giving any member or employee of the Company, or any person whomsoever, any legal or equitable right against the Company, the Committee or the Trustee, unless such right shall be specifically provided for in this Plan or conferred by affirmative action of the Company, in accordance with the terms and provisions of this Plan.

APPENDIX B.
SAMPLE PERFORMANCE
SHARES PLAN

FUNDAMENTAL PHILOSOPHY

The purpose of this Plan is to stimulate executive level performance for the benefit of XYZ Corporation and the proposed objectives by which senior management will be measured on an individual basis must serve that purpose or they are invalid as legitimate measurements. To get 100% of the assigned incentive, we should set our objectives to *exceed* budget and to attain outstanding performance. Therefore, throughout this proposal the attainment of the 1973 budget will achieve less than the maximum incentive award allocation. A second fundamental strategy has been the criterion that no incentive award for 1973 will be considered earned, even on a minimal basis, until 1972 has been exceeded. The objectives set for 1973 must of necessity be tied to budgets and shares already established. Therefore, these proposals are intended for one year only. For 1974 and later years, it is our intention to move in the direction of company growth percentage goals and divisional growth percentage goals for sales and profitability.

We have classified our employees to be rewarded by this plan, as follows:

A. Employees who will be assigned worldwide performance objectives.
B. Employees who will be rewarded on the bases of International Division performance.
C. Employees who will be rewarded on the basis of performance in Domestic Divisions:

1. Receivables.
2. Inventories.
3. Manufacturing Controllable.
4. Sales.

D. Emphasis on Special Divisions:

1. Research and Development.
2. Quality Assurance.
3. Legal.
4. Treasury.

By way of illustration, let us look at employees who will be given world-wide performance objectives:

1. *Pretax earnings:*

1973 budget plus 5% equals $17,900,000 equals 100% bonus.
1973 budget equals $17,079,000 equals 90% bonus.
1973 budget minus 10% equals $15,371,000 equals 70% bonus.
1973 budget minus 20% equals $13,663,000 equals 50% bonus.
1973 budget minus 30% equals $13,400,000 equals 25% bonus.
Below $13,400,000—zero bonus.

2. *After-tax earnings:*

1973 budget plus 10% equals $18,508,000 equals 100% bonus.
1973 budget equals $16,825,000 equals 90% bonus.
1973 budget minus 10% equals $15,132,000 equals 50% bonus.
1973 budget minus 20% equals $13,459,000 equals 25% bonus.
There will be no bonus for after-tax earnings under $13,459,000.
After-tax profits must show an improvement over 1972 of 15% before executive incentive bonus will commence (see charts 41 and 42).

XYZ CORPORATION
1973 PERFORMANCE UNIT PLAN

1. Purpose

The purpose of the Plan is to benefit XYZ Corporation through increased incentive on the part of key employees (including officers) of XYZ Corporation and its subsidiaries and to aid XYZ Corporation in retaining its present management and, should circumstances require it, to attract additions to the management.

2. Administration

The Plan shall be administered by a committee composed of not less than three members of the Board of Directors (the Board) designated by the Board. No

Chart 41.   Incentive Based on Worldwide Pretax Profit Performance (1973 only)

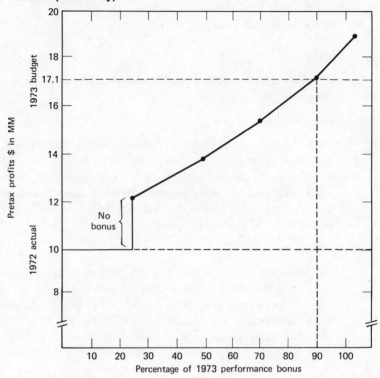

member of such committee, while serving as a committee member, shall be eligible to receive any grant under the Plan. Decisions and determinations by the committee shall be final and binding upon all parties, including XYZ Corporation shareholders, participants and other employees. The committee shall have the authority to interpret the Plan, to set up and revise rules and regulations relating to the Plan and to make any other determinations which it believes necessary or advisable for the administration of the Plan. Subject to the terms and conditions of the Plan, the committee shall have exclusive jurisdiction (a) to select the employees to be granted Performance Units, (b) to determine the number of Performance Units covered by each grant, (c) to determine the time or times when Performance Units will be granted, (d) to determine the time or times, and the conditions subject to which, any amounts may become payable with respect to Performance Units, (e) to fix the payment dates of each grant, and (f) to prescribe the form of the instruments evidencing any Performance

**Chart 42.   Incentive Based on Worldwide Aftertax Profit
Performance (1973 only)**

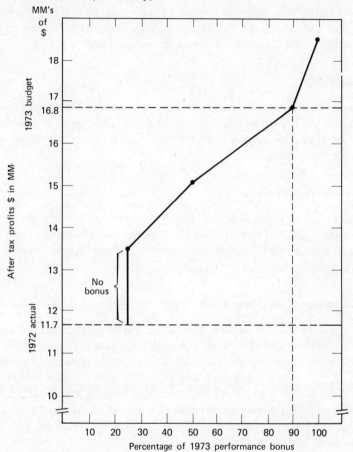

Units granted under this Plan. The conditions subject to which any amounts
may become payable with respect to any Performance Units may be based upon
such considerations as the committee may deem in the best interests of XYZ
Corporation, including but not limited to, the results of operations of XYZ Corporation and one or more of its divisions, subsidiaries, and units and length of
participation in the Plan and may be different for different participants. In taking action under this Plan, the committee shall consider the recommendations
of such of XYZ Corporation's executive officers as the committee may deem
appropriate.

3. Number of Performance Share Units

The committee may make grants for an aggregate of 400,000 Performance Units, plus such additional Units to which grants may be authorized by adjustments made by the committee pursuant to section 6 hereof.

4. Eligibility

Performance Units may be granted to key employees of XYZ Corporation and its subsidiaries (including officers and directors who are also employees of XYZ Corporation or a subsidiary of XYZ Corporation). A participant may receive more than one grant.

5. Limitation on Awards

No grants shall be made under this Plan subsequent to December 31, 1977.

The total number of Performance Units included in all grants to any participant shall not exceed 10% of the total number of Performance Units for which grants may be made under this Plan.

6. Adjustment in Case of Changes in Stock

In the event of any subdivision or combination of the outstanding shares of XYZ Corporation Common Stock, by reclassification or otherwise, or in the event of the payment of a stock divided, a capital reorganization, a reclassification of shares, a consolidation or merger, or the sale, lease or conveyance of substantially all the assets of XYZ Corporation, the Board shall make appropriate adjustments in the number of Performance Units theretofore granted to participants and in the aggregate number of Performance Units for which grants may be made under this Plan.

7. Payments

No payments will be made to participants prior to 1974. The amount to be paid to each participant on any payment date shall be the fair market value on the date of payment of his Performance Units with respect to which payment is to be made on such date. Payment shall be made wholly in cash or wholly in shares of XYZ Corporation Common Stock, valued at their fair market value on the date of payment, or partly in cash and partly in shares at the discretion of the committee. Shares delivered on any payment date may be either treasury shares or authorized and unissued shares or both. For purposes of this section, the "fair market value" of a Performance Unit or a share of XYZ Corporation Common Stock on a particular date shall equal the average of the closing prices on the New York Stock Exchange during the 30-day period preceding such date for a share of XYZ Corporation Common Stock.

Payment shall be made as soon as reasonably practicable after the end of the period which determines a participant's right to receive such payment, provided that the committee may make such exceptions to the foregoing as would be in the best interests of XYZ Corporation.

In making awards the committee may provide that the transfer of any shares of XYZ Corporation Common Stock delivered in payment may be restricted for up to three years from the date of payment, although such shares shall be fully vested in and nonforfeitable by the holder thereof.

8. Right to Payment

A participant shall have no right to receive payment for any part of his Performance Units and all of his Performance Units shall be forfeited unless he remains in the employment of XYZ Corporation or its subsidiaries at all times from the date of grant of the award through the date as of which performance is to be determined in accordance with the terms of the award. Also, the committee may, if in the opinion of the committee circumstances warrant such action, approve payment to which a participant does not have a right as a result of his failing to remain in the employment of XYZ Corporation or its subsidiaries for the required period.

9. Nontransferability

Amounts payable under the Plan shall be transferable only by will or by the laws of descent or distribution.

10. Death, Disability, or Retirement of Participant

Should a participant die, become disabled, or retire before payment to him in full with respect to Performance Units awarded to him under this Plan, the committee shall have the discretion to make payment.

11. Substitute Grants

The Committee may substitute restricted stock grants or other forms of awards for Performance Units if in the opinion of the committee such substitution would result in more favorable tax consequences to the participant or XYZ Corporation or for other reasons, which, in the opinion of the committee, make such substitution desirable. Notwithstanding the foregoing provisions of this section, the committee shall not substitute any other form of award for Performance Units unless, in the opinion of the committee such substitution would not result in any significant increase in the cost of the Plan to XYZ Corporation. Any such opinion of the committee may be based upon such considerations as the committee may deem appropriate including, but not limited to, the fair market value of a Performance Unit on the date such substitution is made.

12. Voting and Dividend Rights

No participant shall be entitled to any voting rights or to receive any dividends with respect to any Performance Units.

13. Securities Act

Each participant will represent that all shares of XYZ Corporation Common Stock received in payment are acquired for his own account for investment and not with a view to the resale or other distribution thereof, and non of such shares will be transferred by a participant except in accordance with such conditions as shall satisfy the General Counsel of XYZ Corporation as being in compliance with the Securities Act of 1933 and the rules and regulations thereunder.

14. Miscellaneous Provisions

No employee or other person shall have any claim or right to be granted an award under this Plan. Neither this Plan nor any action taken hereunder shall be construed as giving any employee any right to be retained in the employ of XYZ Corporation or any of its subsidiaries.

XYZ Corporation shall have the right to deduct from all awards paid in cash any taxes required by law to be withheld with respect to such cash awards and, in the case of awards paid in XYZ Corporation stock, the employee or other person receiving such stock shall be required to pay to XYZ Corporation the amount of any taxes which XYZ Corporation or any of its subsidiaries is required to whithhold with respect to such stock.

15. Cancellation of Performance Units

In addition to cancellation by forfeiture as a result of failure to complete the requisite period of employment or failure to earn payment by meeting performance objectives, the committee may cancel Performance Units with the written consent of an employee holding such Performance Units granted to him under the Plan. In the event of any cancellation, all rights of the former holder of cancelled Performance Units in respect of such cancelled Units shall terminate, and such Units shall be available for further grant in accordance with the Plan.

16. Amendments and Termination

The Board of Directors may at any time terminate this Plan or amend it, provided that no such action shall adversely affect any right or obligation with respect to any award theretofore granted nor increase the number of Performance Units covered hereby.

17. Effective Date of the Plan

This Plan shall be effective as of January 1, 1973.

APPENDIX C. SAMPLE PENSION PLAN UMBRELLA OVER SOCIAL SECURITY AND DEFERRED PROFIT SHARING

**RETIREMENT PLAN
FOR HOURLY EMPLOYEES OF
XYZ CORPORATION AND
PARTICIPATING COMPANIES**

ARTICLE I DEFINITIONS

Section 1.1 Definitions and Construction of Terms

The following words and phrases when used herein shall have the following meanings unless a different meaning is plainly required by the context:

(1) "XYZ" shall mean XYZ Corporation.

(2) "Company" shall refer individually to XYZ and subsidiaries, affiliates and other corporations associated under the Plan. Any subsidiary, affiliate or other corporation associated with XYZ or any division, department or similarly identifiable unit of any such corporation shall have the right, with the consent of the Board of Directors of XYZ to participate in this Plan.

(3) "Participating Unit" shall mean a division, department or similarly identifiable unit of a participating Company as the Board of Directors may, from time to time, designate as eligible to participate in the Plan. Subject to the provisions of any applicable collective bargaining agreement, the Board of Directors shall have the right at any time and from time to time to include or withdraw from the Plan the participation of any division, department or similarly identifiable unit of a Company.

(4) "Date of establishment" shall mean January 1, 1967.

162

(5) "Employee" shall mean an employee of a Company.

(6) "Service" shall mean continuous service with a Participating Unit. The Committee may, at any time or from time to time, by uniform rules classify as "service" for purposes of this Plan service rendered to any predecessor corporation of a Company or any other present or past corporation related to or associated with XYZ or predecessor thereof. In computing for the purpose of any provision of this Plan the number of years or months of service of an employee, there shall be included the period of a leave of absence not in excess of one year, absence because of sickness, service in the Armed Forces or Government of the United States, periods recognized as service under an applicable collective bargaining agreement, and other types of absence uniformly approved by the Committee for all employees.

(7) "Credited service" shall mean completed years and months of continuous service beginning on the first day of the month following completion of six months of service by an employee and ending on his Normal Retirement Date.

(8) "Board of Directors" shall mean the Board of Directors of XYZ.

(9) "Compensation" shall mean the total earnings paid by the Company to an employee during each calendar year of credited service, exclusive of payments made pursuant to the cash profit sharing plan of the Company.

(10) "Beneficiary" shall mean the person or persons designated as beneficiary by an eligible employee on a form to be prescribed by the Committee and filed with the Committee; and shall mean the legal representative of the estate of such employee in the case of the lapse or failure of such designation.

(11) "Trust Fund" shall mean the Trust established pursuant to this Plan out of which benefits provided by this Plan shall be paid.

(12) "Trustee" shall mean the Trustee of the Trust Fund.

(13) "Committee" shall mean the Retirement Plan Committee as provided in Section 4:2.

(14) In computing periods of time hereunder, credit will be given for each completed month of service and a fractional part of a month shall be disregarded.

(15) The masculine gender shall include the feminine, and the singular shall include the plural.

ARTICLE II   ELIGIBILITY

Section 2.1   Eligibility

Any employee of the Company shall be eligible to participate in the Plan if:

(A) He is employed in a Participating Unit.

(B) He has completed at least six months of continuous service.

(C) He is compensated on an hourly basis.

Provided, however, that an eligible employee in a collective bargaining unit represented by a labor union shall participate only when there is in existence an agreement making the Plan available to eligible employees in such unit.

Section 2.2 Suspension of Participation

In the event an employee ceases to meet the eligibility requirements of Paragraph (A) or (C) of Section 2.1 for any reason other than termination of employment, his participation in the Plan shall be suspended and no further contribution shall be made by the Company on his behalf until he again qualifies under such requirements. A suspension of participation shall not constitute a break in continuous service but the period of suspension shall not constitute credited service in computing the value of the benefits, if any, payable under the Plan upon such employee's subsequent termination of employment.

ARTICLE III EMPLOYEES' BENEFITS

Section 3.1 Normal Retirement Date

The Normal Retirement Date of an employee shall be the last day of the month in which he attains age 65, at which time his employment shall cease.

Section 3.2 Amount of Normal Pension

An eligible employee retired pursuant to this Plan at Normal Retirement Date shall be entitled to an annual pension equal to:

(A) The sum of the following credits:

(1) In the case of an employee who was covered under the Plan on the date of establishment, a past service credit consisting of (a) 1% of his compensation for the year ended December 31, 1966, multiplied by the number of years and months of his credited service with the Company prior to January 1, 1967, and prior to his attaining age 50, and (b) 2% of such compensation, multiplied by the number of years and months of his credited service with the Company prior to January 1, 1967, and after he had attained age 50.

(2) A future service credit consisting of 1% of his compensation for each year of his credited service after January 1, 1967.

(B) Less the sum of:

(1) The amount which would be payable to the employee if his Deferred Profit Sharing Benefit (as hereinafter defined) were paid to him in equal monthly installments for life upon the actuarial assumptions used in determining the benefits and contributions to this Plan.

(2) Fifty percent of the amount of the Primary Benefit to which the employee would be entitled in accordance with the provisions of the Federal Social Security Act, as amended through the year 1965.

For purposes of computing an employee's pension benefit under the foregoing formula, the term "Deferred Profit Sharing Benefit" shall mean that portion of the amount accumulated for his benefit at Normal Retirement Date under the Deferred Profit Sharing Plan for Hourly Employees of XYZ Corporation and Participating Companies which is attributable to the minimum percentage deferrable on his behalf in accordance with the schedule of Company contributions set forth in Section 4 of the Deferred Profit Sharing Plan.

Section 3.3   Duration and Payment of Pension

A pension shall be paid to a retired employee so long as he shall live, in monthly installments on the last day of each month commencing on the last day of the month next succeeding the date of his actual retirement and ending upon the last day of the month next succeeding the date of such employee's death.

Section 3.4   Optional Forms of Benefit Payment

In lieu of the normal form of pension payments prescribed by Section 3.3, an eligible employee may elect to convert the pension otherwise payable to him at Normal Retirement Date into a pension of equivalent actuarial value in accordance with one of the following options:

Option A.   A reduced pension benefit payable during his lifetime, with the provision that after his death 50%, 66⅔%, or 75%, or 100% of his reduced pension benefit (as he shall specify) will be continued during the life of such person as he shall have designated in his written notice of election.

Option B.   A reduced pension benefit payable during his life with the provision that, if the employee should die before receiving at least 60 or 120 payments (as he shall specify), payments will be continued to his beneficiary for the balance of the specified period.

The election of an optional form of pension or any change therein shall be made in writing delivered to the Committee on such form as the Committee may prescribe and must be accompanied by evidence satisfactory to the Committee of the employee's good health unless such election is made at least one year prior to Normal Retirement Date. If an election is made under either of the foregoing options and the employee's designated beneficiary dies prior to the employee's Normal Retirement Date, the election shall be ineffective.

Section 3.5   Effect of Termination of Employment

An eligible employee whose services with the Company are terminated for any reason, other than total and permanent disability, prior to his Normal Retirement Date and before attaining age 55 and completing 10 years of credited service shall have no right to any benefit under the Plan. In the event an employee's services are terminated for any reason other than death, total and permanent disability, or retirement at Normal Retirement Date and after having attained age 55 and completing 10 or more years of credited service, he shall be entitled to a pension benefit computed in accordance with the provisions of Section 3.2 on the basis of his credited service prior to such termination of employment. The benefit so determined shall be paid to the employee commencing at his Normal Retirement Date as provided in Section 3.3 and shall be subject to the optional forms of benefit payment as provided in Section 3.4. In lieu of receiving such pension benefit in the form of a deferred pension commencing at Normal Retirement Date, an employee may, with the consent of the Committee, elect to receive the actuarial equivalent of such benefit commencing on the last day of the month next succeeding the date of his termination of employment determined in accordance with such actuarial tables as the Committee may adopt.

Section 3.6   Total and Permanent Disability

In the event the employment of an employee is terminated prior to Normal Retirement Date due to total and permanent disability, he shall be entitled to a pension benefit computed in accordance with the provisions of Section 3.2 on the basis of his credited service prior to such termination of employment. The benefit so determined shall be paid to the employee, commencing on the last day of the month next succeeding the date of his termination of employment, as provided in Section 3.3 and shall be subject to the optional forms of benefit payment as provided in Section 3.4.

The term "total and permanent disability" shall mean a medically determinable physical or mental impairment of at least six months' duration which renders the employee unable to engage in any substantial gainful activity and which can be expected to result in death or to be of long-continued and indefinite duration. The fact of total and permanent disability shall be determined in the sole judgment of the Committee and such determination shall be conclusive.

Section 3.7   Death of Employee

In the event the services of an eligible employee are terminated by death prior to Normal Retirement Date, no payment will be made under the Plan on behalf of such employee. The benefit, if any, payable upon the death of a former employee after Normal Retirement Date will depend upon the optional form of benefit payment elected by the employee prior to his retirement in accordance with Section 3.4 of the Plan.

Section 3.8   Company's Option with Respect to Small Payments

When any benefit hereunder becomes payable, if the amount is less than $20.00 per month, the Trustee may in its discretion make payment at quarterly intervals or, with the consent of the Committee, liquidate the entire liability hereunder by paying the then actuarial equivalent as determined by the Company in a lump sum.

ARTICLE IV   ADMINISTRATION OF THE PLAN

Section 4.1   The Trust Fund

Any and all rights which may accrue under this Plan shall be subject to all of the terms and provisions of any Trust Agreement which XYZ may enter into with respect to the Trust Fund, which Trust Agreement, upon its execution, shall be deemed to be part of this Plan.

Section 4.2   Retirement Plan Committee

The general administration of the Plan and the responsibility for carrying out the provisions thereof shall be placed in the Retirement Plan Committee consisting of five members appointed by the Board of Directors to hold office during the pleasure of the Board. The members may, but need not, be employees of a Company. The books and records of the Committee shall be made available at all reasonable times to any collective bargaining agent representing an eligible employee.

The Committee may employ or appoint agents, counsel, accountants, actuaries, and such clerical and other services as it may require in carrying out the provisions of the Plan.

The Committee shall have the exclusive right (except as to matters reserved to the Board of Directors under the Plan or which the Board of Directors may from time to time reserve to itself) to interpret the Plan and to decide any and all matters arising thereunder. All decisions of the Committee in respect of any matter hereunder not reserved to the Board of Directors (and all decisions of the Board of Directors on matters reserved to it) shall be final, conclusive, and binding upon all persons having or claiming to have any right or interest in or under the Plan.

The Committee from time to time shall adopt service and mortality tables for use in all actuarial calculations in connection with the Plan and shall determine the rate of interest to be used in such calculations. As an aid to the Committee in adopting tables and in determining the amount of contributions required from year to year, the actuary selected by the Committee shall make periodic actuarial studies of the assets and liabilities of the Plan and shall recommend to the Committee tables and rates of contribution. The Committee shall in turn recommend to the Board of Directors the rate of contributions to be made by each Company from year to year.

The Committee, the Board of Directors, each Company and their respective officers shall be entitled to rely upon all tables, valuations, certificates, and reports furnished by any actuary, upon all certificates and reports made by any accountants, and upon all opinions given by any legal counsel, in each case duly selected by the Committee in accordance with the provisions of the Plan. The members of the Committee, of the Board of Directors, each Company and their respective officers shall be fully protected in respect of any action taken or suffered by them in good faith in reliance upon any such tables, valuations, certificates, reports, or opinions, and all actions so taken or suffered shall be conclusive upon each of them and upon all persons having or claiming to have any interest in or under the Plan. The members of the Committee shall use ordinary care and diligence in the performance of their duties but no member shall be personally liable by virtue of any contract, agreement, bond or other instrument made or executed by him or on his behalf as a member of the Committee; nor for any mistake of judgment made by himself or any other member of the Committee, nor for any negligence, omission, or wrongdoing of any other member or of anyone employed by the Committee, nor for any loss unless resulting from his own gross negligence or willful misconduct.

Section 4.3   Determination of Disputes between a Company and an Employee or Beneficiary

If at any time any dispute shall arise between the Company and an employee, either before or after retirement, or any beneficiary designated by an employee or who claims to have been so designated, such dispute shall be determined by the Retirement Plan Committee, whose determination thereof shall be final and conclusive and binding upon all persons having or claiming any interest thereunder or in the Trust Fund.

ARTICLE V   CONTRIBUTIONS, AMENDMENT, AND DISCONTINUANCE OF THE PLAN

Section 5.1   Contributions

Contributions to provide the benefits under the Plan shall be made by the participating Companies to the Trustee at such time and in such amounts with respect to each Company as shall be determined by the Board of Directors consistent with the terms of any applicable collective bargaining agreement. In addition, the Companies shall contribute all expenses of administering the Plan, including the compensation of the Trustee. Forfeitures arising from severance of employment, death, or for any other reason shall not be applied to increase the benefits any employee would otherwise receive under the Plan at any time prior to the complete discontinuance of contributions by the Company by which he is employed. Amounts arising from such forfeitures shall be used to reduce the Company's contributions hereunder.

Section 5.2   Company's Right to Amend or Discontinue Plan

It is the intention of XYZ and the other participating Companies to continue this Plan indefinitely and to make such contributions as may be required hereunder regularly each year. Nevertheless, subject to the provisions hereinafter set forth and to the provisions of any applicable collective bargaining agreement, XYZ reserves the right, at any time or from time to time, by action of its Board of Directors to modify or discontinue the Plan in whole or in part or to reduce, suspend or discontinue contributions hereunder; provided that no such action may be taken which, by reason thereof:

(1) Will deprive any employee, retired employee or his beneficiary without his consent of any benefit theretofore accrued to him with respect to contributions theretofore made under the Plan; or

(2) Shall make it possible for any part of the corpus or income of the Trust established pursuant to the Plan to be used for, or diverted to, purposes other than for the exclusive benefit of employees, retired employees, or their beneficiaries under the Plan prior to the satisfaction of all liabilities with respect to such employees, retired employees and their beneficiaries.

Notwithstanding the foregoing provisions or any other provision of this Plan, any modification or amendment of the Plan may be made, retroactively if necessary, which XYZ deems necessary or appropriate to conform the Plan to, or to satisfy the conditions of, any law, governmental regulation or ruling, and to permit the Plan or Trust to meet the requirements of the Internal Revenue Code.

Section 5.3   Distribution of the Trust Fund on Discontinuance of the Plan

In the event of the termination of the Plan, or upon the complete discontinuance of contributions thereto, the assets of the Trust Fund shall first be allocated to each participating Company in proportion to the aggregate value of the accrued pension benefits of the employees of each Company, adjusted in the case of any Company for years in which contributions were reduced or suspended by that Company. Thereafter, the assets so allocated to each Company shall be used to provide the pension benefits accrued under the Plan to the date of termination or complete discontinuance of contributions for that Company's eligible employees and their beneficiaries in the following order:

First.   To provide the pension benefits under the Plan for all retired employees and disabled employees receiving pension benefits.

Second.   To provide the pension benefits in accordance with the provisions of Section 3.5 of the Plan for or on account of active and former employees who have attained age 55 and have completed ten or more years of credited service.

Third.   To provide the pension benefits under the Plan for or on account of the other active employees to the extent of the value of their respective benefit credits which have accrued to them at the date of termination of the Plan or the complete discontinuance of contributions.

Fourth.   The balance, if any, arising as the result of erroneous actuarial computations during the previous life of the Plan and remaining after the sat-

isfaction of all liabilities for pension benefits accrued under the Plan prior to
the date of termination with respect to employees, retired employees, and
their beneficiaries, if any, shall be returned to the Participating Unit.

In making the provisions required in this Section 5.3, assets which the Committee shall deem sufficient shall first be allocated to provide in full the benefits
of each class before allocating any assets to any subsequent class. If the remaining assets are insufficient to provide in full for the benefits in any class,
the benefits of all retired or active employees and beneficiaries of that class
shall be reduced pro rata. The Committee shall instruct the Trustee as to the
application of assets in accordance with the provisions of this Section.

ARTICLE VI   EFFECT OF THE PLAN

Section 6.1   Nonalienation of Benefits

All benefits payable hereunder are for the sole use and benefit of the participating employees and their beneficiaries and, to the extent permitted by law,
shall be free, clear and discharged of and from, and are not to be in any way liable for debts, contracts, or agreements now contracted or which may hereafter
be contracted, and from all claims and liabilities now or hereafter incurred by
any participating employee or his beneficiary or beneficiaries. No employee, or
beneficiary hereunder, shall have the right to commute, anticipate, withdraw,
surrender, encumber, alienate, or assign any of the benefits to become due
hereunder unto any person or persons upon any terms whatsoever.

Section 6.2   Limitation of Rights

Neither the establishment of the Plan, nor any modification thereof, nor the creation of any fund, trust or account, nor the payment of any benefits shall be
construed as giving any employee of the Company, or any person whomsoever,
any legal or equitable right against the Company or the Trustee, unless such
right shall be specifically provided for in the Trust or the Plan or conferred by
affirmative action of the Trustee or the Company in accordance with the terms
and provisions of the Plan; or as giving any employee of the Company the right
to be retained in the service of the Company; and all employees shall remain
subject to discharge to the same extent as if the Plan had never been adopted.

ARTICLE VII   WITHDRAWAL OF A COMPANY

Section 7.1   Withdrawal by XYZ

XYZ may, upon 30 days' written notice, request a participating Company to withdraw from the Plan and upon the expiration of such 30-day period, unless such participating Company has taken the appropriate corporate action to accomplish such withdrawal, such Company shall be deemed to have withdrawn from the Plan and the provisions of Section 7.2 hereof shall apply. The Committee shall give written notice to the Trustee of any such withdrawal.

Section 7.2   Withdrawal by Participating Company

Any participating Company may withdraw from the Plan by giving the Committee 30 days' written notice of its intention to withdraw. In the event any such Company withdraws from the Plan, the Committee shall thereupon determine that portion of the Trust Fund which represents, with respect to the employees of such Company, an amount which bears to the Trust Fund the same ratio which the actuarial reserve for the employees of such Company bears to the total actuarial reserve in the Trust Fund. The Committee shall thereupon instruct the Trustee to set aside such assets in the Trust Fund as the Committee shall specify which equal in value that portion of the Trust Fund so determined by the Committee. The Committee in its discretion shall direct the Trustee either (1) to hold such assets so set aside for the exclusive benefit of the employees of the withdrawing Company who were members of this Plan on the date of such withdrawal, or (2) to deliver such assets to such Trustee or Trustees as shall be selected by such withdrawing Company.

If the withdrawal of a Company from this Plan has the effect of a termination of the Plan so far as such Company and its employees are concerned, or in the event of a complete discontinuance of contributions to the Plan by a participating Company, then, in either event, the rights of such Company's employees, retired employees, and their beneficiaries shall be governed by the provisions of Section 5.3.

If the Company which ceases to participate in the Plan and which withdraws its pro rata share of the assets from the Trust Fund continues the Plan or adopts a substantially similar plan for the benefit of its employees, the withdrawal from this Plan by that Company shall not be regarded as a termination of the Plan so far as that Company and its employees are concerned; the provisions of Section 5.3 shall be deemed inapplicable; and the rights of such Company's employees, retired employees, and their beneficiaries shall be governed in accordance with the provisions of the Plan so continued, or substantially similar plan so adopted, by such Company for their benefit as if no withdrawal from this Plan had taken paace.

ARTICLE VIII   INTERNAL REVENUE SERVICE APPROVAL

Section 8.1   Internal Revenue Service Approval

The establishment of this Plan and Trust is subject to the condition precedent that the Plan and Trust shall be approved initially by the Internal Revenue Service as meeting the requirements of the Internal Revenue Code of 1954 and the regulations issued thereunder with respect to employees' plans so as to permit the Companies to deduct, for income tax purposes, the amount of their contributions to the Trust pursuant to the Plan, and so that such contributions will not be taxable to the eligible employees as income. Accordingly, notwithstanding any provisions herein to the contrary, prior to obtaining such approval by the Internal Revenue Service, no rights shall vest in any employee or beneficiary under the Plan or Trust, no payment shall be made to any employee or beneficiary from the Trust, and, if such approval is not obtained, the funds, if any, theretofore contributed by any Company shall be returned to it and the Plan and Trust shall thereupon be terminated.

Index